What Comes Next?

A Preliminary Bibliography of Recent Proposals For a Different Society, With Critical Annotations

by Thad Williamson

National Center for Economic and Security Alternatives
Washington, DC
February 1997

2000 P Street, NW, Suite 330
Washington, D.C. 20036
U.S.A.

Printed in the United States of America by P.A. Hutchison, Inc.

ISBN 0-934560-00-5

Dedicated to the memory of Professor William Gerald McLoughlin (1922-1992), in gratitude for his most important teaching: How to learn from the past, struggle in the present, and hope for the future.

Contents

Acknowledgments . . . . **p. v**

Preface—by Gar Alperovitz . . . . **p. vii**

Chapter One: **Globalization, the Decay of Liberalism,
and the Mainstream Policy Debate** . . . . **p. 1**

I. Introduction and Overview

II. Annotations

    a. William Wolman and Anne Colamosca
    b. William Greider
    c. Jeff Faux
    d. Robert Kuttner
    e. Paul Krugman
    f. Robert Reich
    g. Lester Thurow
    h. John Kenneth Galbraith
    i. Robert Bellah
    j. Michael Sandel
    k. E.J. Dionne
    l. William Julius Wilson
    m. Michael Lind
    n. Tony Blair
    o. David Imbroscio
    p. Michael Shuman
    q. Susan Meeker-Lowry
    r. Barbara Brandt

III. Additional References

Chapter Two: Market Socialism .... **p. 43**

I. Introduction and Overview

II. Annotations

    a. Leland Stauber
    b. David Miller
    c. John Roemer
    d. James Yunker
    e. Tibor Liska
    f. Marton Tardos
    g. David Schweickart
    h. Michael Albert and Robin Hahnel
    i. Pat Devine
    j. David McNally
    k. Michael Barratt Brown
    l. Alec Nove
    m. Thomas Weisskopf, Samuel Bowles, and David Gordon
    n. Curtis Moore
    o. Wlodzimierz Brus and Kazimierz Laski
    p. Arjun Makhijani
    q. Thomas Pogge
    r. N. Scott Arnold
    s. Christopher Pierson

III. Additional References

Chapter Three: Sustainability and the System Question .... **p. 87**

I. Introduction and Overview

II. Annotations

    a. William Ophuls
    b. Rudolf Bahro
    c. Andre Gorz
    d. Lester Milbrath
    e. Hazel Henderson

Contents

    f. Herman Daly and John Cobb
    g. Douglas Booth
    h. Ted Trainer
    i. Juliet Schor
    j. David Pepper
    k. Larry Rasmussen
    l. Murray Bookchin
    m. Gar Alperovitz

III. Additional References

Chapter Four: Utopian Literature . . . . **p. 127**

I. Introduction and Overview

II. Annotations

    a. Callenbach's *Ecotopia*
    b. LeGuin's *The Dispossessed*
    c. Russ's *The Female Man*
    d. Piercy's *Women On the Edge of Time*
    e. Delany's *Triton*
    f. Atwood's *The Handmaid's Tale*
    g. Wagar's *A Short History of the Future*
    h. Robinson's *Pacific Edge*

III. Additional References

Chapter Five: Additional Visions . . . . **p. 143**

I. Introduction and Overview

II. Annotations

Nonacademic visions:
a. Alfred Andersen
b. J.W. Smith
c. Margrit Kennedy
d. Sam Smith

Philosophical Perspectives:
e. Iris Marion Young
f. Phillipe Van Parijs
g. Joshua Cohen and Joel Rogers
h. E.M. Adams
i. John Dryzek
j. Thomas Naylor and William Willimon
k. Nancy Fraser

Theological Perspectives:
l. Harold Wells
m. Gary Dorrien
n. Michael Lerner
o. Ulrich Duchrow

III. Additional References

Acknowledgments

This bibliography is a product of the ongoing work of the National Center for Economic and Security Alternatives in Washington, DC. The Center wishes to thank the board of the French American Charitable Trust, and in particular, Diane Feeney, for its support of this project. Additional, much appreciated support was also received from one anonymous donor.

The germ of this book began in 1993 as a research memorandum written for the President of the National Center, Gar Alperovitz, and this bibliography benefits chiefly from the opportunity to work with Dr. Alperovitz on "The Good Society" Project for the past five years. It also benefits from the cumulative research and work of NCESA staffers past and present. I am particularly indebted to former staff members Dawn Nakano and Hany Khalil for helping introduce me to the literature reviewed herein, and to current staffer Alex Campbell for helping keep me up to date with the most recent material.

George Williamson assisted in identifying and providing brief annotations of a number of relevant German and French thinkers who have not yet been translated into English; work with French and German language sources was then carried forward by Seth Richards, Claire Lyddall, and Marien Ferdinandusse. This work-in-progress on foreign language sources will be fully incorporated into future editions of the bibliography.

Ted Howard assisted in planning the production of the hard-copy version of the bibliography, which was designed by Stacy Swartwood. Andrea Brunholzl copy-edited the manuscript and suggested many helpful improvements in the text.

Numerous persons provided feedback on earlier drafts of the bibliography, or provided useful references to add to the bibliography. In this regard, I am particularly appreciative of the feedback of Curtis Moore and the many references and pertinent intellectual discussions provided by the Progressive Economist Network electronic mailing list (Pen-L).

E.M (Maynard) Adams and Michael Shuman graciously assisted the project by agreeing to provide me with manuscripts of their books in advance of publication.

I am also grateful for the staff assistance and access to resources provided by numerous libraries over the course of this research, including the Gelman Library at George Washington University; Suzzalo Library at the University of Washington; Lauinger Library at Georgetown University; the Burke Library of Union Theological Seminary; Low Library at Columbia University; Davis Library at the University of North Carolina, Chapel Hill; Dupont Library at the University of the South; and the Library of Congress.

Finally, the production of this volume was assisted immensely by the encouragement, intellectual exchange, and practical support leant by my partner, colleague, and best friend, Adria Scharf.

Preface

by
Gar Alperovitz

President, National Center for
Economic and Security Alternatives

By now it is a commonplace that Americans have lost trust in some of the nation's most important institutions: Public belief in the democratic nature of government—and in the integrity of business leaders, unions, the media, health-care providers, educational leaders, and religious leaders—has declined dramatically since the early 1960s. Observers on both left and right have suggested that below the apparent media calm a subterranean "crisis of confidence" is underway—or even, plausibly, the beginnings of a "delegitimation crisis." At the same time, economic growth, although positive as of this writing, has been slower in the past quarter century than in the postwar era—and sharply increased income inequality has accompanied slower growth. With certain exceptions, ecological problems have also generally worsened in the past quarter century.[*]

In the early years of the postwar era an outside observer might have expected that this confluence of problems and political disillusionment would fuel a significant politics of reform and of renewed social movements. Instead, social movements remain generally weak and national politics remains substantially stalemated, impervious and often hostile to new ideas for reform—especially ideas for progressive reform.

Plentiful (if low paying and insecure) jobs may be the explanation—at least for the time being. However, standing back from the current "moment" of politics to reflect upon other historical eras characterized by stalemate and loss of belief, one might also expect the emerging context to begin to generate a deeper "rethinking" of long term vision and strategy: With traditional pathways blocked, the alternative is a continuation of current failing strategies and the abandonment of traditional progressive values.

---

[*] See *The Index of Environmental Trends*. Washington: National Center for Economic Alternatives, April 1995.

It is not often realized that such a rethinking effort is not only underway, but that there has been a massive outpouring of new ideas, new visions, new conceptions of long-term political-economic goals, and in general the emergence of a rich and diverse literature which is laying intellectual groundwork for what might plausibly one day give rise to a renewal of positive strategic development. Just below the surface of media attention one finds responses to the main features of the new era we have entered: The decay of the welfare state, the collapse of Soviet-style socialism, the accelerating process of economic globalization, a diminution of effective nation-state sovereignty, growing ecological crises around the world, increasing inequality both within and between nations, racial, gender and ethnic conflicts. Progressive political-economic and ecological writers have been stimulated (indeed, forced!) to begin to articulate an alternative vision of politics, economics, and community life for the new century. There is also a broader academic literature, and a sophisticated dialogue which transcends traditional political positions among some of the nation's leading political theorists, economists, and sociologists.[*] The trajectory of current institutional difficulties has also engendered new debate amongst thoughtful conservative intellectuals. Inevitably, some visions are partial; others attempt to be comprehensive; some are aimed at producing immediate political results; others look to long-term prospects.

Thad Williamson's bibliography is an attempt to capture, contextualize, and bring into dialogue a careful selection from several diverse strands of progressive thought. The central question posed in this literature concerns the nature of a coherent alternative to the dominant political and economic systems of the twentieth century: corporate capitalism and state socialism. And, too, how (or if) it might be possible to make meaningful progress towards realizing such a vision. It should be obvious that the writers here assembled do not agree that "history is over"—that traditional capitalism has triumphed, that it is the be-all and end-all of all history. At one level, the writers implicitly ask of those who think the current moment of history represents all that there will ever be: Do you truly believe that the systems which happen to exist just now will last *forever*? At another level, they stand in the tradition of those who throughout history have "made history"—i.e.,

---

[*] See, for instance, *The Good Society*, the journal of the Committee on the Political Economy of the Good Society, University of Maryland at College Park.

viii

the people like, say, the early American revolutionaries, who at the outset seemed to be without significant support but who somehow represented something new, something powerful. In recent years societies from the former Soviet Union to South Africa have learned that the apparent stability of existing institutional patterns is rarely the end of history—and nations as different as France, India, China, Mexico, and many many others know this from their own developmental history.

This is not to say that the various forms of capitalism which currently dominate national development will inevitably be replaced by some future alternative system. It is simply to suggest extreme caution—and the danger of mistaking the seeming solidity of current power for (often implicit) theories of historical inevitability which subtly transform what is into what always must be: What the future may hold, quite simply, is unknown.

If there is ever to be serious movement in the direction of more equitable, democratic and ecologically sustainable political-economic systems, there will clearly also have to be: a sense of shared values upon which to base future social and institutional life; a proximate, defensible, and coherent, even if necessarily incomplete, vision of how a system of political, economic, and social institutions designed to support such values might function in the real world; a sense of immediate strategies and policy steps which might plausibly move over time in the appropriate direction; and, finally, communities of people joined together to make things happen. Williamson's main goal in the following pages is not to summarize the full range of thought on all these issues; rather it is to highlight and evaluate key presentations which contribute to the discussion of the structure of a long term alternative. The summaries, accordingly, mainly focus on ideas pertaining to the second and third of the above requirements—i.e., the nature of new institutions which might ultimately fulfill such values as liberty, equality, democracy, community, and ecological rationality; and proximate steps which might be taken to build institutions which can nurture such values.

This bibliography represents one of a series of practical and theoretical undertakings at the National Center for Economic and Security Alternatives. The perspective and analytical stance are informed by ideas which have been developed over the last ten years in seminars and research efforts—and by surveys of "on-the-ground" institutional development. The bibliography is intended to serve as an introductory guide to the emerging literature and also as a discussion and evaluation of the particular strengths, weaknesses, and overall contributions of each writer from the perspective of this overall effort.

A central assumption in what follows is that a democratic alternative for the new century must emerge from a democratic process: no one thinker or group can possibly have "all the answers." Our hope is that this attempt to begin to catalogue and evaluate the growing number of serious alternative proposals will contribute to a further democratization of intellectual and political work—and to a far-ranging and ever deepening dialogue about what the future might become: We desperately need our own modern form of Federalist debate about the constitution of society in the new century. Finally, and above all, we hope this bibliography will help readers develop their personal understanding—and, too, their own visions, theories and practical strategies for positive long-term change.

Chapter One

Globalization, the Decay of Liberalism, and the Mainstream Policy Debate

Introduction and Overview

This initial chapter provides a necessarily selective review of recent policy literature produced by prominent liberal, communitarian, and progressive intellectuals. The guiding question behind the analysis and discussion in this chapter is, "What are the policies and reforms a sympathetic American political party might implement to best forward the ideals of more equality, more democracy, better environmental health, and stronger communities?" This question is related to, but ultimately quite different from, the topic occupying the subsequent four chapters: "What is the concrete institutional structure of 'the good society', and is there a way to get there?" Nonetheless, it is a useful exercise to examine up front the "reformist" literature, both as a source of particular insights and proposals, and as a way of mapping the way various progressive thinkers have responded both to the rightward shift in American politics and the larger trend of an increasingly market-dominated global economic system.

It is virtually a truism to say that liberals and progressives of all stripes have been swimming against the grain in American political culture since the late 1970s (with the possible exception of a very brief moment of hope after Bill Clinton was elected President in 1992 on a "Putting People First" agenda). Less often noted are the changed tones in which the most prominent voices of American liberalism speak—changed tones which reveal the full measure of this rightward swing.

Perhaps the most striking case is that of Robert Reich, one of the most energetic promoters of liberal economic policies in the 1980s, who in 1991 published *The Work of Nations,* a major statement on how American economic policy should respond to the reality of globalization. The major thesis of that book is that government should concentrate on developing the

1

skills of its workforce in order to make America as attractive a site as possible for investment by transient multinational corporations. However, as Secretary of Labor in the first Clinton Administration, Reich quickly learned that bond-market priorities would severely limit attempts to provide significant new federal investment in workers' skills. Reich's lively recounting of his experience as liberal advocate within an "Eisenhower Republican" administration, 1997's *Locked in the Cabinet*, has the feel of a defeated soldier's commentary on the war. Placed in its political and historical context, that book serves as a powerful caution to liberal thinkers in general: Do not underestimate the formidable power of the interests of the status quo, which can frustrate even the best-laid plans of would-be reformers.

This pessimism is reflected, explicitly or implicitly, in several other works reviewed in this chapter: Robert Kuttner, editor of *The American Prospect*, a leading journal of liberal policy discussion, directs his attention in *Everything for Sale* to defending the idea of a mixed economy against the onslaught of wholesale free marketers; Jeff Faux, head of the labor-supported Economic Policy Institute, tries to insist that the Democratic Party can be something other than a business-sponsored enterprise in his book *The Party's Not Over*; Harvard economist Paul Krugman weighs in with critiques of both supply-side economics and "pop internationalist" policy entrepreneurs (including both Kuttner and Faux)—but in the end appears more or less resigned to accepting persistent inequality and slow economic growth as the only achievable outcomes in a modern-day capitalist economy.

This is not to say that critique of dominant free-market models is not important work in itself; Kuttner's latest book is a particularly effective answer to many of the most frequently repeated nostrums of mainstream economics regarding the "virtues" of markets. But Kuttner and others in the present discourse serve politically as voices of dissent, not as voices of a freshly ascendant political paradigm. We have traveled far from the golden age when forthright liberals such as Arthur M. Schlesinger Jr. and John Kenneth Galbraith could play leading roles in setting the tone for discussion of national affairs. If this were not the case, it would hardly be necessary, with Kuttner, to publish a 400 page refutation of the idea that "everything should be for sale."

To be sure, there continue to be many other books which follow the conventional formula of first providing analysis and critique of the existing economic policies, and then an exposition of recommended policy changes intended to rectify the problems. Several such works are reviewed here. But as liberal ideas have been mostly rejected at the national level of power for over 20 year, such works have become increasingly ineffective in their capacity to shape public discourse, much less public policy itself, as a growing number of writers are acutely aware. Lester Thurow, for instance, who once envisioned a society in which ratios of inequality between the top and bottom of the economic ladder were reduced to no more than five-to-one and, as recently as 1992, proposed active European-style labor market and industrial policies as the key to rejuvenating America, in his most recent book simply despairs of ever correcting long-term trends in inequality within the paradigm of "capitalism." Similarly, journalist William Greider concludes his recent, firsthand account of how the global market is operating by suggesting that political change to correct the emerging reality may be decades away—and will require much more fundamental institutional change than the current policy debate is prepared to discuss.

This annotated bibliography takes as a starting point the last observation noted by Greider: Conventional attempts to achieve substantive political change through national-level policy are at an impasse, a "stalemate," for the foreseeable future. A stalemate does not mean that what goes on in Washington is irrelevant or can be ignored, but a context in which traditional progressive ideas have little chance of being implemented ought to force left-of-center thinkers, activists, and citizens to consider the question: If the architecture of power characteristic of the present-day American political economy does not allow substantive reform in the direction of basic social values (such as decent economic prospects for all), might it be necessary to build, however slowly or however difficult, an entirely different "system" of power, if such values are ever to be realized? The attractive idea of being able to simply vote the right candidate or party into national power and implement positive reforms remains alluring—but as Reich's very visible experience suggests, it is a weak strategy for bringing traditional progressive values such as liberty, equality, community, democracy, and ecological sustainability to life. While surely there is much to learn from the books reviewed in this initial chapter, perhaps the most interesting feature to note in the ensuing discussion is how various writers characterize the political implausibility of their own best, and in many cases quite admirable, policy proposals.

This chapter concludes on a somewhat different tack from the national-level approach to policy reform by reviewing four policy thinkers—David Imbroscio, Michael Shuman, Susan Meeker-Lowry, and Barbara Brandt—who focus on building local-level alternatives. Examining their proposals will serve as a useful segue into the discussion of full-fledged systemic alternatives.

William Wolman and Anne Colamosca. *The Judas Economy: The Triumph of Capital and the Betrayal of Work*. New York: Addison-Wesley, 1997.

Wolman, chief economist at *Business Week* magazine, and Colamosca provide a straightforward indictment of "globalization" and the political triumph of the interests of capital in the developed capitalist countries, with particular focus on the fate of workers (and by extension everyday life) in the United States. Their charge: The growing mobility of capital, which has placed American workers in direct competition with increasingly skilled workers in the south, together with restrictive, anti-inflation oriented monetary policies, has created a regime of slow economic growth, increased inequality, and growing stress and insecurity for workers and their families. If left unchecked, the authors state, these trends will create a new "crisis" of capitalism—possibly in the form of a global "deflation" or depression that will eventually topple not only workers' incomes, but the sky-high stock market on which many Americans have pinned their long-term financial hopes.

By way of policy response, Wolman and Colamosca offer a traditional Keynesian set of strategies focused on increasing government investment in education, infrastructure, and technological development at the national level; pro-growth monetary policies; and a high degree of cooperation among developed economies' governments to rein in capital. They also promote increased unionization, making it easier to change jobs and relocate (in contrast to the idea of economically stabilizing community in particular places), and most interestingly, a sort of "job insurance" payoff for workers who lose their jobs via downsizing that would be far more generous than traditional unemployment programs and would protect laid-off workers against total financial devastation.

Like most business writers, the authors do not engage ecological concerns at all; and by making the well-being of American workers their sole test of policy, they at times fall prey to a narrow nationalism, implying that workers in developing countries are getting a break at developed nations' expense by living in countries which are permitted by the world financial establishment to pursue rapid growth policies.

4

This book is aimed squarely at policy elites, and the authors show little hope of their agenda being adopted by either party: One of the book's concluding statements is the rather whimpering observation that "[T]he real lesson of the 1990s is that the threat of global deflation is far more credible than the threat of a resurgence of global inflation. We can only hope that the policy establishment recognizes these new realities soon." [1] In fact, the more likely outcome by far is that Wolman and Colamosca's advice will be roundly ignored, and that present negative trends will continue. However, the authors have provided a useful service in outlining the likely negative consequences, in a strictly economic sense, of maintaining the present policy course. Indeed, the picture of economic pain they paint will likely form the context in which efforts to begin constructing an entirely different kind of economy must begin.

William Greider. *One World, Ready or Not: The Manic Logic of Global Capitalism*. New York: Knopf, 1997.

On the basis of hundreds of interviews with a wide variety of policy makers, bankers, speculators, corporate executives, workers, and activists from across the globe, Greider paints a picture of a world economy spinning out of control, in serious danger of being consumed by its own contradictions. How is it, he asks, that the real time it takes to manufacture an automobile has fallen by over 50 per cent in the last 20 years—and yet the number of paychecks it takes for an average American family to buy a car has risen by a third? What is the world to make of China, whose continuing development could swallow huge amounts of the developed world's corporate capital, with devastating effects on what remains of the the manufacturing sector in those countries?

From the American point of view, Greider sees the crisis as threefold. First, like everyone else, the nation is confronted with the fact that with capital increasingly mobile, jobs do disappear to more hospitable business climates. Second, unlike most everyone else (particularly Asian nations), the American government has no strategy for setting rules on corporate capital or for preserving a stable, nationally rooted industrial capacity. Thirdly, America is currently playing an unsustainable role as the world's "buyer of last resort" via its massive trade deficit with the rest of the world, a deficit that in Greider's view is slowly dragging down the value of the American economy. Greider proposes a "social tariff"—a tariff intended to penalize countries which do not respect labor rights or maintain effective environmental standards—to help combat that deficit and to provide an incentive to poorer nations to raise their labor and environmental standards.

Greider's analysis is sprinkled with attacks on mainstream economic theory: He argues, for instance, that many trade relocations—such as Boeing agreeing to shift production to China in exchange for long-term contracts—are flat-out political deals, not responses to the "market," and that the cause of historically high interest rates in the 1990s is not a shortage of capital and capacity, but a paucity of "good borrowers." The book's central argument, however, is that the world as a whole now faces conditions similar to those precipitating the Depression in America: a productive over-capacity, whereby industry can produce much more than can be sold. This situation causes industries to close factories and layoff workers, which in turn depresses consumer demand, and so on. Greider cites the example of the worldwide auto industry, which has the capacity now to produce 70 million vehicles a year but can only sell 47 million of them.

What is needed, Greider argues, is a "floor" of basic working and living conditions for the poorest of nations, thus ending the savage race to the bottom which characterizes capital's search for ever-cheaper labor. Possible mechanisms would be a global minimum wage, as well as the social tariff. Greider also argues for numerous top-down restrictions on corporate capital and on the operations of global financial markets, and a drastic shift in monetary policies to promote faster economic growth. Specific proposals include providing debt relief for less developed nations; applying the "Tobin" tax on capital flows across borders to discourage purely speculative activity; banning capital transfers from offshore banks; reforming subsidy policy (such as the activities of the Export-Import Bank) to favor domestic job creation; raising taxes on corporations and finance capital and instituting a wealth tax; and instituting global labor standards as a prerequisite for participating in trade.

Greider is unusually forthright in calling for the United States to raise trade barriers against nations like Japan that maintain "irregular mercantilist practices that exact zero-sum advantage at the expense of trading partners. Those economies that persist in accumulating huge trading surpluses would lose their cost-free access to foreign markets through emergency tariffs or other measures." [2] This step would initiate movement towards a balanced global trade regime, where major players maintained a rough match between exports and imports.

Beyond these nearer-term policies, Greider also endorses a form of Louis Kelso's plan to make all workers and citizens owners of corporation. By using Treasury money to loan workers the money to buy shares in corporations, dividends from those shares would allow eventual repayment of the Treasury money (plus interest), making workers and citizens the effective owners of corporate America. Greider also discusses the possibility of firms directly owned by local level governments, with all citizens as "shareholders," entitled to a share of the profit stream.

cf. Green Bay Packers

Greider gives some attention in the closing chapter to the views of Herman Daly on developing a truly ecologically sustainable economy, and to the possibility of creating "closed loop" industrial enterprises that might drastically increase the job base of industrial production. However, Greider's ecological concern is clearly subordinate to his desire to see a global-style Keynesian economic boom that would first lift up the lowest living standards.

Reaction to this book from professional economists has been mixed at best. Paul Krugman maintains, contrary to Greider, that trade has played a relatively small role in the loss (to date) of American manufacturing jobs, and he has challenged Greider's use of some statistics. Lester Thurow has endorsed many of Greider's policy prescriptions, but argues that the current free-market craze will pass in time. Thurow also finds Greider inconsistent in citing both a rentier-oriented monetary regime and over-capacity as drags on the global economy, and argues that over-capacity should lead to the rich consuming more of their own income, which would in turn re-stimulate consumer demand. While neither line of criticism is conclusive or entirely persuasive, both Krugman and Thurow's dissents point to the need to accumulate more empirical and anecdotal evidence to support Greider's over-capacity thesis, if it is to gain wide acceptance as an explanatory model of what is going on in global capitalism.

Jeff Faux. *The Party's Not Over*. New York: Basic Books, 1996.

Jeff Faux focuses on the need for liberal Democrats to develop a new political and economic "story" capable of building majority support for progressive economic policies. Yet Faux also believes that "there are no fundamentally *new* stories in politics." What is proposed then is simply an updating and extension of the New Deal story. After attacking both the story of supply-side economists, and even more forcefully, that told by "New Democrat"-style centrists in the Democratic Party, Faux proposes two basic themes to guide a "liberal economic nationalist" project. The first theme, "You Are Not Alone," says that the bottom 75% of the workforce should not be abandoned but in fact privileged by economic policy. The second theme, "Rebuild America First," stresses the idea that policy should aim to build up infrastructure, decaying cities, and so forth at home first in order to create a path of fast economic growth and rising wages, with sharply increased public investment as the key lever. The basic elements of Faux's proposed policies (quoted verbatim below) are familiar:

- A commitment to sustained full employment by lowering interest rates and targeting investments in people and infrastructure
- Empowering workers by removing restrictions on the right to bargain collectively and by raising the minimum wage
- Resolving the budget crisis through national health care
- Widening corporate responsibility beyond shareholders
- Reforming the tax code
- Promoting international labor rights and Third World debt relief as a first step toward regulating the global economy.[3]

Faux would create a separate capital budget to fund the increased public investments, possibly giving special advantages to corporations that meet standards of investing in domestic plants and job training (along the lines of New Mexico congressman Jeff Bingaman's "A-Corps" proposal). He also urges the need to renegotiate NAFTA and to begin implementing international controls on capital flows and corporate behavior.

Faux admits in the last chapter of the book that the deck is heavily stacked against this agenda, but goes on to sketch a scenario whereby this "story" might regain hegemony within the Democratic Party and eventually capture national power:

- Reconstruction of the grassroots infrastructure of the once-proud Democratic Party. To make this happen, Faux suggests launching many local and state-level discussions of the future—discussions which inevitably favor the concepts of government and planning over laissez-faire approaches. This process might help raise the "expectations" of the public, leading to an exploration of an alternative to the stagnant, slow-growth economic track;
- Revitalization of labor union strength under John Sweeney
- Bringing environmentalists on board for an "economic nationalist agenda"

- Politicizing minority groups with a working-class consciousness that transcends identity politics
- Making a major ideological push to relegitimize the idea of government
- Passage of campaign-finance reform.

It is excusable to characterize this scenario as more of a wish list than a reading of likely political trends. Faux does not seem to face up to the problem posed by John Kenneth Galbraith: If you add up all the traditional liberal constituencies together, you still do not get a political force capable of shaking the residual political power of the "contented classes." Indeed, Faux, like many other liberal writers, simply bypasses serious discussion of the history of twentieth century political and economic development in the United States, a history that casts serious doubt on the capacity of progressive electoral politics to achieve structural reforms sufficient to alter long-term income distribution trends in the absence of crisis or war.

In the end, Faux's strongest argument is simply a logical one: The Democratic Party cannot neglect its traditional constituencies forever without going out of business. Eventually those constituents will abandon the party, either by embracing third party efforts or simply by staying home on Election Day. This is a legitimate, persuasive point. But to state that the party will likely slowly die without adopting Faux's new story should not equate to an expectation that the party will be wise enough to follow Faux's lead; it is likely, even probable, that the Democrats will simply continue to deteriorate as a force for progressive change, with no other large-scale actor to take its place on the national scene for some time to come.

Robert Kuttner. *Everything for Sale: The Virtues and Limits of Markets.* New York: Knopf, 1997.

Kuttner's very substantial book walks through many of the current debates in economics and public policy, all the while debunking conservative ideas about the unique capacity of the unguided market to produce economically efficient and socially desirable outcomes. After a quick sprint through 50 years of economists' ideas about the nature of markets, Kuttner takes up the issues of the labor market, health care, the financial world, the relationship between markets and technological development, regulation, and the influence of money in politics, in each case using numerous real-world examples to illustrate that some form of government intervention or restraint upon the market is urgently justified. The end result is both an accumulation of convincing, common sense arguments against everyday conservative punditry and yet another laundry list of policy proposals to correct the present infatuation with unfettered markets.

Kuttner' approach to labor markets reveals a sense of the overall method at work. He notes that labor markets are the one area of economic life in which economists traditionally have agreed that factors other than supply and demand are highly salient in the setting of "prices." Employee-employer relationships take place within an institutional context over an ongoing period of time, and employers cannot monitor and precisely reward the actual productivity of workers, which varies from person to person, week to week, hour to hour. Companies must pay attention to the "social character of work" and create a social environment that provides enough security to workers to make ongoing productive work possible. Thus, employers commonly pay above-market rate salaries to workers in order to maintain their loyalty and prevent them from constantly entertaining outside offers. Kuttner notes, however, that the era of downsizing, independent consultants and overall increased job insecurity has made the real-world labor market more and more like a traditional market, a trend Kuttner views as ominous. He goes on to note that even in the present climate some corporations continue to stick to a "high-road" strategy of high security for employees, and that it might yet be possible to create a new "social labor market." The problem is not economics, but politics, and the lack of a political mobilization to force a new social contract.

Taking up the familiar problem of increased wage inequality among workers in the United States, Kuttner cites several causes, including insufficient purchasing power which has helped create a "global imbalance of supply and demand;" high unemployment, which undercuts the bargaining power of workers; the decline of manufacturing and the rise of the service economy; weakened minimum wages; industry deregulation which has inspired waves of corporate cost-cutting; and the decline of union power. Taking on Robert Reich and others, Kuttner downplays the significance of the "skills mismatch" in the United States as an explanation of rising inequality, stating that "it is simply not true that industry abruptly raised the hurdle in terms of the skills required to hold a good job. Rather, given the weakness of labor's bargaining power and the flood of displaced blue-collar workers, industry was simply able to draw from a higher-educated pool of applicants for the same old jobs." Kuttner further argues that the overall skill and educational level of American workers has been steadily rising, yet workers have not been rewarded with increased wages as productivity has improved: "In the absence of other changes that would reverse the bargaining asymmetry between labor and industry, it is very unlikely that the human-capital solution would change these patterns in the distribution of earnings." [4]

The elements of a reconstructed social labor market, then , would be full employment, increased subsidies for low wages (like the Earned Income Tax Credit), stronger unions, fair trade agreements, improved education and training, encouragement of long-term deals between management and labor, and possibly special benefits for grade "A" socially responsible corporations (along the lines of the Bingaman proposal). Kuttner similarly ends his succeeding chapters with these policy recommendations:

- A universal coverage health care system that creates incentives to pursue preventive care and upgrade public health
- The Tobin tax on stock transactions which might encourage corporations to hold longer time-horizons and discourage speculation
- An active post-Cold War policy for using government's proven research capacity to stimulate technological development, in partnership with industry
- Re-regulation of the airlines, on the grounds that regulatory regimes help markets operate more efficiently
- A defense of "social regulation" policies
- A call to renew the political process by removing the sway of money over campaigns and policy-making.

Kuttner is unusually stimulating in reaching these conclusions—for instance, he provides a devastating indictment of the negative impact of airline deregulation on consumers—yet the analytic insight and wisdom provided here has the feel of an against-the-tide plea for common sense in the wake of negative political trends, a cry of despair that wrongheaded thinking could be so ascendant. The best Kuttner can offer by way of a scenario in which his proposed policies might come to center stage is to suggest that at some point a backlash to the "market utopia" idea is inevitable, and to hope that in some unspecified way political activity may become "more effective" as the "emblem of a free democratic people" and that the electorate might become "engaged and informed." [5]

11

Paul Krugman

Pop Internationalism. Cambridge: MIT, 1996.
Peddling Prosperity. New York: W.W. Norton, 1994.

Having attained fame in the 1980s with his work on strategic trade theory and his highly regarded attacks on apologists for Reaganomics, MIT international economist Krugman in recent years has staunchly attacked the proposition that "globalization" is a foremost cause of the decline in American manufacturing and wages. In *Pop Internationalism*, Krugman demonstrates that less than one-fifth of the decline in the manufacturing sector since 1970 can be attributed to the trade deficit in manufacturing. Somewhat less convincingly, Krugman also argues that "factor price convergence," the tendency of prices for labor worldwide to converge as globalization proceeds, is not a significant factor in declining American wages. The real culprit? Technological progress, which has reduced the cost of manufacturing goods and allowed employers to eliminate unneeded jobs. At the same time, however, low overall economic productivity has helped keep wages down. The long-term solution to improving wages, Krugman says, must be increased productivity.

It is possible to agree with Krugman that the sheer impact of trade has been overestimated and still raise questions about his overall conclusions. If increased productivity invariably leads to increased wages, why have wages risen less than one-third as fast as productivity since 1980? Unlike some of the writers (such as Kuttner) whom he fiercely attacks, Krugman makes little mention of the shifting institutional context of the American labor market, such as declining unionism and a shrinking minimum wage, as a cause of lower wages. Similarly, while Krugman shows that net investment by American corporations to date in the Third World is still a small percentage of GDP, he ignores the possibility that the very threat of such corporate relocations has substantially increased the bargaining power of capital vis-a-vis labor.

Krugman argues that the goals of economic policy should be modest: To ameliorate but not "solve" the problems of low productivity and high poverty. Krugman has thus called for health care reform, regulatory reform, and deficit cutting (in order to raise productivity) and more spending on anti-poverty programs as the heart of a modest economic agenda that avoids doing harm. Something of a deficit hawk, Krugman is no fan of Keynesian spending to stimulate productivity and thereby lift wages; nor does Krugman speak much about restoring the balance between capital and labor, or making educational investments to increase long-term productivity. While Krugman's analyses are sharp, Kuttner is correct to point out in a recent *American Prospect mano a mano* exchange with Krugman that the latter's writings leave liberal economists without a coherent public philosophy. Indeed, it is difficult not to conclude that Krugman believes nothing substantial can be done to restructure "the economy," and that if this is not perhaps the best of all possible worlds, it's probably impossible to get to a significantly better one without doing something perverse along the way.

Robert Reich

The Work of Nations. New York: Knopf, 1991.
Locked in the Cabinet. New York: Knopf, 1997.

Reich was a prominent critic of Reaganomics from a progressive liberal perspective throughout the 1980s, and he received wide attention for his 1991 book *The Work of Nations.* That book decried the trend towards an unequal, two-tiered American society, in which "symbolic analysts" prospered while traditional blue-collar and unskilled workers suffered. Reich postulated that the top-fifth of American society was on the verge of essentially seceding from public life; those who could afford to pay for private services would drop political support for public goods, leading to an increasingly polarized society. Reich's primary proposed antidote to this trend, in addition to the usual support for more progressive taxation, was to sharply increase investment in the skills and education of the bottom 80% of society, so that workers would be prepared to prosper in an era of little job security. The country as a whole would then become a magnet for corporate investment in high-tech, high-paying jobs.

A longtime friend of Bill Clinton's, Reich is the rare policy writer who got the opportunity to attempt to put his ideas into practice as Secretary of Labor between 1993 and 1996. Reich's recounting of that experience, *Locked in the Cabinet*, is a frank admission that Clinton's program utterly failed to redress the trend of growing inequality and underinvestment in human capital. Reich details the gutting of Clinton's public investment program, and the failure of Clinton to pass either health care reform or striker replacement legislation. He decries the obsequiousness towards Wall Street interests which characterized Clinton's key economic decisions, and the unswerving hand with which Federal Reserve chair Alan Greenspan has pursued a rigidly anti-inflation, slow growth monetary policy.

Reich came to Washington with the idea of brokering a "grand bargain" between "Save the Jobs"-type traditional liberal constituencies and his pro-free trade, neoliberal colleagues by getting organized labor to go along with NAFTA in exchange for striker replacement legislation and increased job training spending. But Reich soon learned that such a bargain was simply impossible politically. After the 1994 election, Reich was the last declared liberal in the Clinton cabinet, and he correctly takes a large share of the credit for passing a $.90 increase in the minimum wage and for helping make corporate welfare and sweatshop labor national issues. At the same time, Reich despairs of his friend the President signing the 1996 welfare bill, and attacks the increasing influence of pollsters like Dick Morris who are more interested in packaging then governing. Finally, Reich points to the entrenched power of private business interests in Washington and their effect on both parties. The shift in Reich's perspective from this experience is apparent near the end of the book when he comments favorably on the election of John Sweeney as the new President of the AFL-CIO:

> American politics and much of American economics ultimately come down to a question of power—who has it and who doesn't. The widening economic gap is mirrored in a widening gap in political power within our society. I came to Washington thinking the answer was simply to provide people in the bottom half with access to the education and skills they need to qualify for better jobs. But it's more than that. Without power, they can't get the resources for good schools and affordable higher education or training. Powerless, they can't even guarantee safe workplaces, maintain a livable minimum wage, or prevent sweatshops from reemerging. Without power, they can't force highly profitable companies to share the profits with them. Powerless, they're as expendable as old pieces of machinery.[6]

Along the way, Reich provides some interesting quotations and dialogues describing the power realities of Washington. Reich quotes former House Budget Committee chair Martin Sabo, a Minnesota Democrat, describing the congressional Democrats this way in March of 1993:

> We're owned by them. Business. That's where the campaign money comes from now. In the nineteen-eighties we gave up on the little guys. We started drinking from the same trough as the Republicans. We

figured business would have to pay up because we had the power on the Hill.... We were right. But we didn't realize we were giving *them* power over *us*. And now we have both branches of government, and they have even more power. It's too late now.[7]

In December of 1994, Reich describes the cool reception his proposals to combat corporate welfare received among his fellow Oval Office advisors:

[Clinton] tells me he's intrigued by the theme of corporate welfare and the possibility of saving billions of dollars a year that could be used for new investments. But my colleagues are less than enthusiastic. At today's budget meeting I suggest to them we finance the education and training tax break by closing some tax loopholes. In deference to Bentsen I avoid any mention of oil and gas. What about the tax breaks for the insurance industry?

Bentsen: That would be *very* unwise, politically.
Stephanopoulos: Republicans would accuse of raising taxes.
Panetta: The insurers would be on top of us.
Rubin: The financial markets would take it badly.
Bentsen: Don't even *think* about it.

I gingerly offer up another one: The advertising industry claims that advertising builds up a company's goodwill with customers for years, right? So take them at their word. Prevent companies from deducting the entire cost of their advertising right away. Make them treat advertising like any other investment and deduct its cost over several years. This would save the Treasury billions.

Panetta: *Advertisers*? Are you *kidding*? We'd have the media all over us.
Bentsen: A nonstarter.
Stephanopoulos: Forget that one. And don't repeat it outside this room.
[Laughter.]
Rubin: The financial markets would take it very badly.[8]

Although the accuracy of some of Reich's recollected conversations has been challenged, the bottom line value of Reich's book remains. Here is an honest liberal admitting that his best efforts, while not without effect, failed to make a dent in the larger direction of the country—and that there is little reason to suspect that Washington-based decision makers will be able to make such a dent in the foreseeable future.

15

Lester Thurow. *The Future of Capitalism*. New York: William Morrow, 1996.

The author of numerous popular books describing the "big picture" of American and international economic life, Thurow here spells out the contours of capitalism's trajectory in Europe, Japan, and the United States, with a primary focus on the intractable problem of inequality: Thurow declares that "No country not experiencing a revolution or a military defeat with a subsequent occupation has probably ever had as rapid or as widespread an increase in inequality as has occurred in the United States in the past two decades." [9] Thurow cites not a skills mismatch, but what he describes as a uniquely American gap in skills between the university-educated top and the "third world" skills of the bottom as the primary culprit in this inequality, adding in other factors such as slow growth, factor price equalization, union weakness, deregulation, demographics, and the increasing percentage of labor compensation devoted to pension payments, not wages. After spending the bulk of the book exploring these possible explanations, the author returns near the end of the book to ruminations on "Democracy Versus the Market."

Thurow's concern is that without another competing social system to make capitalist societies attuned to their own faults, there will be little political impetus to make the large-scale public investment in the public goods—particularly education and infrastructure—needed for capitalism to thrive. Thurow points out that

> For more than twenty years earnings gaps have been rising, and for more than ten years that reality has been known with certainty. Yet the political process has yet to adopt its first program to change this reality. The problem is of course that any program that might work would have to involve a radical restructuring of the American economy and American society. More money is required but an aggressive program of reeducation and reskilling the bottom 60 percent of the workforce would require a fundamental painful restructuring of public education and on-the-job training. Without a social competitor, fear will not lead capitalism to include the unincluded. Long-run enlightened self-interest should lead to the same result, but it won't. [10]

The result, Thurow predicts, will be a long period of stagnating economies and diminishing belief in democratic processes, creating a welcoming climate for political demagogues to emerge. Thurow calls on parties of the left to reformulate a "utopian" vision that recasts the idea of a "common good" as the antidote to increasing privatization and chaos. Thurow draws analogies to the Middle Ages as another era where private goods displaced public goods, leading to the breakdown of civilization and a period of virtual barbarism. Thurow is frankly pessimistic, noting that "Internal reform is very difficult in capitalism, since it has a set of beliefs that deny the need for conscious institutional reforms." [11]

Thurow's attempt at a hopeful conclusion, a call for the advanced capitalist societies to somehow recreate a "Builder's Ideology" that emphasizes long-term investment in the future and inclusion of all, seems oddly out of step with the stark realities so skillfully posed in his penultimate chapter. But Thurow is helpful—and novel—in stating that an alternative vision to capitalism must be developed, if capitalism is to undertake the reforms needed to ensure its own healthy future.

John Kenneth Galbraith

The Good Society. Boston: Houghton Mifflin, 1996.
The Culture of Contentment. Boston: Houghton Mifflin, 1992.
A Tenured Professor. Boston: Houghton Mifflin, 1989.

Harvard economist emeritus Galbraith has maintained his substantial presence in liberal intellectual life with three notable books in the past ten years. The earliest, *A Tenured Professor,* is a whimsical novel with a serious point: The protagonists of the novel, a young, Ivy-educated couple, decide that the problem with liberals is that they don't have enough money; then, after the husband has attained tenure at Harvard, they devise a system for calculating the precise irrationalities of Wall Street trading by which certain stocks are wildly overvalued. By using this knowledge to sell short on stocks, the couple makes first a tidy bundle and then a huge fortune in the Wall Street crash of October 1987. The couple uses this new found financial power to launch a series of bold progressive initiatives, including a product labeling system describing firms' policies towards women and a takeover of a major television network. This last venture is sufficient to arouse the full interest of government regulators who shut down the couple's illicit trading and force them to give up the empire. While the punch line of the novel is that all this was possible once tenure was granted, Galbraith's fictional scenario of how progressive values might directly confront the mainstream of American culture convincingly demonstrates one crucial point: Lots and lots of money in support of the effort would be needed.

In 1992's *The Culture of Contentment*, Galbraith spells out what he sees as the fundamental structural obstacle to liberal reform: the domination of American politics by a "contented" class, amounting to roughly the top third of society—Galbraith goes so far as to count the contented as the "majority" of voters, which would be some 50 million adults. This class dominates public discourse, provides almost all electoral financing, votes at a much higher rate than lower-class Americans, and hence holds a firm rein on political decision making in America. This is also the class of Americans which is getting along just fine economically; and while members of the class may object to aspects of present political and economic arrangements, these quibbles are not experienced as a matter of direct urgency. Hence, there is predictably strong resistance among the contented to proposals that might hurt their economic position (such as higher taxes). This bias in policy affects the platforms of both major parties, and is the backdrop for the growing trend in social and economic inequality.

Galbraith reckons that the odds are very long that this culture will reverse its course in political and economic affairs. The only scenarios likely to stimulate significant reform are all crises: a new Depression, an eruption of violence and revolt in the inner cities, or an unpopular foreign war. Without placing a high probability on any of these outcomes, Galbraith does suggest that the growing social gulf generated by the politics of contentment could eventually lead to some sort of "shock" to the system. But the system is not likely to correct itself. Indeed, Galbraith closes his book with the solemn epitaph that "In the past, writers, on taking pen, have assumed that from the power of their talented prose must proceed the remedial action. No one would be more delighted than I were there similar hope from the present offering. Alas, however, there is not." [12]

In his 1996 follow-up book, *The Good Society,* Galbraith seems to edge back from the grim conclusions of *The Culture of Contentment.* Having sketched a brief, unsurprising primer for progressive liberalism, i.e. achieving a full-employment economy, high economic growth, ample public goods, and sharp reductions in poverty and inequality via Keynesian spending and pushing for peace, disarmament, and economic uplift of the poor abroad, Galbraith states that a single change in American political culture would suffice to make his program not only possible but even inevitable: drastically increasing the rate of voting among the bottom half of

American society. Regarding the Republican revolution of 1994, Galbraith notes that

> those opposing aid to the poor in its several forms won their stunning victory with the support of less than one quarter of all eligible voters, fewer than half of whom had gone to the polls. The popular and media response was that those who had prevailed represented the view and voice of the public. Had there been a full turnout at the election, both the result and the reaction would have been decidedly different. The sense of social responsibility for the poor would have been greatly enhanced.[13]

An expansion of democracy would lead to a political culture in which the poor could be heard and taken seriously in political decision making.

Galbraith's point is well-taken, indeed even obvious, and there is certainly room for legitimate frustration, voiced publicly in recent years most frequently by Jesse Jackson, that the Democratic Party has not fully appealed to the most likely constituents of a liberal agenda. Yet several crucial caveats to Galbraith's comments on voting need to be raised. First, progressive activists struggled and succeeded in passing Motor Voter legislation in 1993 which has made it much easier for the poor to register to vote and increased voter rolls nationwide. So far, no significant change has resulted in the nation's political culture from this reform. Second, the strong grip corporate interests now hold on congressional Democrats and the Democratic National Committee probably precludes that party from ever changing the basis of its appeals in the direction of the poor, even if several key figures (like Jackson) within the party would sorely like it to do so. If the Democrats will not do so, perhaps another party might; but it would take decades (in the absence of billionaire backing) for a progressive third party to establish itself as a force in national politics. Moreover, a third party scenario surely changes the math underlying Galbraith's analysis; unlike the current Democrats, a third party on the left would have little chance of ever becoming a majority party.

Third, Galbraith probably underestimates the extent to which conservative positions on social issues can cause blue-collar Americans to vote against their economic self-interest: Not everyone added to the rolls from the bottom-third of society would be an automatic vote in the liberal column. Fourth, Galbraith does not consider the possibility that the representatives of the contented, particularly corporate entities, would simply pour more of their resources into the political process at both the legislative and electoral level in response to increased voting rates. As libertarian

Harvard philosopher Robert Nozick has argued, the top 50% of society has both the interest and capacity to attempt to buy off the 51st percentile of voters in order to maintain a majority. Such a dynamic might be expected to operate in the context of a full participation voting polity. Fifth, it should be noted that Galbraith's point has been repeatedly made by various left voices over the past 30 years to little effect. Supporters of this notion probably underestimate the extent to which much of the American population is essentially de-politicized, cut off from politics; the long, difficult task of re-engaging these Americans and convincing them that civic affairs mattered and were worth participating in would probably be a prerequisite for significantly increased voting.

Yet, at another level, Galbraith is fundamentally correct. The ultimate answer to questions about the long-term electoral viability of *any* progressive or left idea is to note that such a program represents the interests of the majority, and hence would be quite viable indeed in situations where strong democracy really existed. While there is good reason to doubt that strong democracy can somehow be established nationally such that a version of Galbraith's extended New Deal liberalism could hold power in the foreseeable future, the long-term relevance of Galbraith's electoral logic cannot be denied.

Robert Bellah, Richard Madsen, William Sullivan, Ann Swidler, and Steven Tipton

The Good Society. New York: Knopf, 1991.
Habits of the Heart. Berkeley: University of California Press, 1985.

Bellah and his co-authors provided the benchmark communitarian critique of evaporating American community and moral purpose with their 1985 work, *Habits of the Heart*. Following up that vastly influential work is the more programmatically minded *The Good Society*, which attempts to spell out in greater substance what a new public philosophy based on a rich democratic vision might look like.

Bellah et al make clear in *Habits of the Heart* that their ultimate hope is in "cultural transformation:"

> The transformation of our culture and our society would have to happen
> at a number of levels. If it occurred only in the minds of individuals (as

to some degree it already has), it would be powerless. If it came only from the initiative of the state, it would be tyrannical. Personal transformation among large numbers is essential, and it must not only be a transformation of consciousness but must also involve individual action. But individuals need the nurture of groups that carry a moral tradition reinforcing their own aspirations. Implicitly or explicitly, a number of the communities of memory we have discussed in this book hold ethical commitments that require a new social ecology in our present situation. But out of existing groups and organizations, there would also have to develop a social movement dedicated to the idea of such a transformation.[14]

In a significant passage, the authors make clear that what they seek is the rebuilding of the idea of community as a way to help modify and reform the existing corporate dominated system.

Reasserting the idea that incorporation is a concession of public authority to a private group in return for service to the public good, with effective public accountability, would change what is now called the 'social responsibility of the corporation' from its present status, where it is often a kind of public relations whipped cream decorating the corporate pudding, to a constitutive structural element in the corporation itself...[15]

The Good Society includes chapters exploring the dilemmas involved in the modern educational system, the "public church," and government possibly contributing to broad cultural change. Regarding the economy, Bellah and associates also point to, but do not fully describe, the need for a positive, institutional structural basis for community: "We need institutional arrangements that enable the relevant publics to recognize the indirect consequences of private economic activities and empower them to regulate these activities for the common benefit..." [16]

Put another way, the "architecture" of Bellah's proposed system looks very much like a corporate capitalist system with the "hope" there will be improved reforms because consciousness has been raised and glued together by a better feeling of community. *The Good Society* is, in fact, rather limited in its specific proposals for remaking economic life, although the goals of corporations and businesses more responsive to the common good and a richer set of public institutions are clear. Better regulation of corporations, support for worker participation in on-the-job decision making, better educated consumers, and maintenance of some sense of "civic equality" in the face of adverse long-term trends round out the authors' economic agenda. While the authors of *Habits of the Heart* and *The Good Society* write insightfully and movingly in both books about the decline of community-feeling in the United States, their proposals to alter the economic patterns driving much of this trend are strikingly modest and imprecise.

Michael Sandel. *Democracy's Discontent*. Cambridge: Harvard University Press, 1996.

Harvard political scientist Sandel, whose 1982 book *Liberalism and the Limits of Justice* stands as a seminal critique of Rawlsian liberalism from a communitarian perspective, here provides an account of the rise and decline of a "political economy of citizenship" in American history. Founding figures such as Hamilton and Jefferson understood that the structure of a nation's economy would play a crucial role in determining the kinds of people and quality of communities that would compose the new country. Concern for the nature of civic life played a guiding role in debates over the political economy in the nineteenth century and into the early twentieth century, when prominent advocates of decentralized communities like Louis Brandeis attacked big business as a threat to democracy and "industrial slavery" working conditions as inimical to the formation of citizens capable of striving for the common good in the public arena.

Sandel produces two stunning quotes from Woodrow Wilson to bolster his case:

> Have we come to a time when the President of the United States or any man who wishes to be the President must doff his cap in the presence of this high finance, and say, "You are our inevitable master, but we will see how we can make the best of it?"

And:

> In all that I may have to do in public affairs in the United States I am going to think of towns, of the old American pattern, that own and operated their own industries. My thought is going to be bent upon the multiplication of towns of that kind and the prevention of the concentration of industry in this country in such a fashion and upon such a scale that towns that own themselves will be impossible.[17]

22

Sandel notes that reformers who preferred a centralist, big-government response to the rise of corporations, such as Theodore Roosevelt and Herbert Croly, also expressed concern for democracy and the character of civic life in forwarding their proposals.

By contrast, political discourse since World War II has hollowed, in Sandel's view, to a narrow type of "procedural liberalism" that emphasizes formal rights and the distribution of goods, but does not ask the fundamental question about whether the political economy is helpful or harmful to civic life. Earlier reformers "were concerned with the structure of the economy and debated how to preserve democratic government in the face of concentrated economic political power. We are concerned with the overall level of economic output and debate how to promote economic growth while assuring broad access to the fruits of prosperity." [18] Sandel believes it is high time to put the older question of how the political economy can support the goals of a democratic civic life squarely on the table.

Specifically, the ideal of community, particularly local community, needs to be re-emphasized and reconstructed; and the narrow conception of "procedural freedom" expanded to a richer definition of "republican freedom" that "consists in acting collectively to shape the public world." Although Sandel does not sketch out a full-fledged program for reviving genuine local communities, he does point out directions for future development distinct from the top-down national reforms proposed by most of the other writers noted in this chapter, even those forwarded by Bellah et al. Sandel argues that more equality is important—but that "civic equality" (the type Mickey Kaus emphasized in his 1991 work *The End of Equality*), as expressed in public spaces, public schools, public libraries, and so forth, are equally important in teaching that rich and poor are all in it together. Looking to local forms of activism, Sandel cites community development corporations, the burgeoning anti-Wal Mart movement, new forms of community design inspired by "New Urbanism," and the Industrial Areas Foundations efforts at community organizing and democratic institution-building as models for defending and reviving concern for community well-being, efforts that seek not just more jobs for the poor, but to build a healthy place to live in the face of larger market processes.

Clearly, Sandel has not solved the problem of how to make the value of community real, given the context of a place-obliterating global marketplace. His book does, however, provide a rich intellectual rationale for some of the more thorough efforts to spell out what the reconstruction of what Sandel terms a "political economy of citizenship" might look like that are noted in the subsequent chapters of this bibliography. One of the few elite political scientists to take notice of on-the-ground bottom-up efforts at social change such as the community development corporation, Sandel has helped crack open the question of "what is the nature of a political economy that could support citizenship, democracy, and community?" in a powerful way with this book.

E. J. Dionne. *They Only Look Dead: Why Progressives Will Dominate the Next Political Era*. New York: Simon and Schuster, 1996.

Written in late 1995, *Washington Post* columnist Dionne's book essentially predicts the downfall of Gingrich-style Republicanism and a political comeback for "Progressive" ideas. Dionne endorses health care reform, creating a capital budget, increased investments in training and education, cutting corporate welfare, reinvigorating unions, expanding free trade (but with protections for workers), "second chance" homes for young single mothers to live with their children in a semi-controlled environment, and other ideas borrowed from Beltway moderate-liberal thinkers. Dionne seeks to reinvigorate the conception of government as a positive moral good, that promotes equality of opportunity and liberty itself, yet at the same time acknowledge that many existing government policies don't work.

Most indicative of Dionne's overall stance, and that of Beltway liberalism in general, are Dionne's thoughts on income equality. "If the link between economic growth and improved living standards is broken, the basic American bargain will be in danger. In the short term, government must be conscious of the problem of falling wages. Its goal would not be massive income distribution. On the contrary, its purpose should be to *prevent* a massive redistribution of income and wealth *away* from the middle class and the poor." [19] This is liberal politics posed in terms of simply resisting the ongoing trends—the thought of achieving substantive equality is not even on the table.

While Dionne is effective in showing that the Gingrich Revolution would have a short half-life, his overall thesis seems to replay the Schlesinger cyclical idea that Gingrich will go down, and therefore the Democrats and Clinton will go up. In fact, as columnist Al Hunt of the *Wall Street Journal* put it in the spring of 1997, despite Clinton's easy re-election both parties seem to be down—and the positive elements of Dionne's "Progressivism" remain in political stalemate. In the end, Dionne's book stands as an unconvincing attempt to put a hopeful, happy face on the unhappy fate of progressive politics on the 1990s.

William Julius Wilson. *When Work Disappears: The World of the New Urban Poor*. New York: Knopf, 1996.

Urban sociologist Wilson provides a thorough descriptive account of how deindustrialization and the loss of well-paying, blue-collar jobs have impacted American ghettoes, creating neighborhoods and entire subcultures in which the idea of productive, remunerative work via legitimate channels is almost unknown. The result is a series of social pathologies, exacerbated heavily by the drug trade, which has attracted the talents of many young poor, largely African-American men in the absence of a viable economic alternative. Altering this reality requires more than economic growth alone. The advance of technology and the potential for outsourcing manufacturing production to the Third World means that jobless, wage-stagnant economic growth is possible; hence, for many American inner cities, the good jobs are gone forever.

Wilson notes that America, unlike Western Europe, lacks the social solidarity needed to undergird a strong welfare-state response to this reality: There is very little sense that all are in it together. At the same time, Wilson acknowledges that the European welfare state model itself is under increasing strain, due in part to rigid nonwage labor costs and high unemployment benefits that make low-wage, American-style service work unattractive to many of the jobless. The quandary then becomes developing both an economic strategy that can create enough well-paying jobs to actually impact inner cities and a political strategy for increasing the amount of services flowing to very poor areas. Wilson recognizes this is nearly an impossible task within the present American political environment: "I...do not advance proposals that seem acceptable or 'realistic' given the current political climate. Rather, I have chosen to talk about what ought to be done to address the problems of social inequality, including record levels of joblessness in the inner-city ghetto, that threaten the very fabric of society." [20]

Wilson's specific proposals include a major public-private effort to raise educational standards (in part by implementing national standards) and to provide European-style vocational training in secondary schools; the expansion of support for child welfare, in particular child care institutions, on the model of the French *ecole maternelle*; increased money for programs aimed at facilitating the "school-to-work" transition for high school graduates; an increase in federal aid to cities to 1980 levels; promotion of central city job creation as the heart of new city-suburb regional cooperation, with particular attention to investments in public transportation; significant expansion of the Earned Income Tax Credit "to lift all poor working families who work full-time year-round out of poverty"; the creation of job information and placement centers in inner cities; providing for "public-sector" employment of last resort to job-seekers; significant increases in public investment in infrastructure to create jobs and help increase economic growth; and finally, following Mickey Kaus, creation of a new version of the Works Progress Administration that would provide both employment of last resort and rebuild public infrastructure.

Wilson has thus spelled out an ambitious social democratic strategy for combating poverty and unemployment. In its major features, the strategy is not different from that pursued by serious liberals over the past three decades: Use the public sector to create jobs directly and promote economic growth, with a special attack on impoverished, job-hungry central cities, and count on improved economic performance to begin to lift all boats. In the long term, similar to Robert Reich's vision, Wilson hopes that preparing "the next generation to move into the new jobs created in the global economy" will mitigate growing wage inequality, and it is reasonable enough to believe that his proposals for stabilizing the bottom—upgrading jobless inner-cities into neighborhood of the working poor—via guaranteed jobs, universal health insurance, the EITC, etc. could put a brake on growing social inequality and decay. Wilson is well aware of the contradictions between this program and what is politically possible in the current legislative environment—and economically possible given the current monetary policies of the United States. Yet, Wilson does no more here than call for "a new political coalition of groups pressing for economic and social reform" to push for his proposed policy framework. Again, little attention is paid to longer-term political obstacles to this program, such as the chronic political weakness of urban interests and the anti-tax bias of suburban voters.

Michael Lind

The Next American Nation. New York: Simon and Schuster, 1995.
Up From Conservatism. New York: Simon and Schuster, 1996.

The decades-old phenomenon of former leftists finding new media fame as reconstructed, ex-Marxist neoconservatives finds an interesting converse in the case of writer Michael Lind. In 1994 and 1995 Lind, formerly a protégé of William F. Buckley, became one of the most prolific writers on the Washington scene precisely as an ex-conservative willing to sharply attack his former allies on grounds of principle. (His current base is *The New Yorker* magazine.) Lind has established himself as an original voice, with a stance echoing in some respects that of the revered historian and cultural critic Christopher Lasch: fierce populism on economic matters, and a celebration of nonelite, working/middle class cultural values. Lind is particularly obsessed with sweeping away racial "preferences" such as affirmative action, which in his view help only a small elite of minorities and alienate working and middle class whites from supporting a progressive agenda. (To his credit, Lind is equally vehement in attacking preferential policies that benefit the "white overclass" such as legacy preferences in college admissions.)

In fact, Lind calls for a renewal of the liberal Democratic tradition of "Roosevelt, Truman, and Johnson" far more passionately than do most of the present-day direct descendants of that tradition. Lind's analysis of the contemporary American political scene is straightforward: There are four primary traditions in American politics, corresponding to the four national candidates in the 1948 presidential election: Far-right conservatism (Thurmond); moderate "neoliberalism" (Dewey): centrist liberal (Truman); and left-liberal (Wallace). Lind equates the present day GOP leadership with the Thurmond contingent of 1948, Bill Clinton with Thomas Dewey's "neoliberalism," and describes the activist core of the Democratic Party as having followed the route of McGovern and Henry Wallace. What is missing, Lind says, is the national centrist liberal tradition, a tradition which he says was correct on all the major issues of the 20th century—the Cold War, civil rights, the mixed economy—yet which has failed to elect a President since 1964 and has fallen off the political map. There are no heirs of Truman left, he declares. (Clearly, Lind exaggerates the point here. What would one call Tom Harkin and Mario Cuomo if not descendants of New Deal liberalism?)

To Lind's mind, what is needed is a revival of a "Nationalism" based on cleaning up politics, launching redistributive economic policies and rebuilding a sense of national identity that transcends racial and ethnic boundaries. (Lind advocates out-and-out assimilationism and hopes, rather implausibly, that one day mixed marriages will render the differences between racial groups as no more significant than those between Americans of Irish and Italian descent.) Practically speaking, such a "Fourth Nationalism" will require a takeover of the Democratic Party, and then the House of Representatives (which Lind considers the nation's most democratic institution). Unfortunately, Lind does not offer a plan for taking back the Democrats from business-backed neoliberalism any more convincing than that offered by, for instance, Jeff Faux.

However, Lind does provide an interesting sketch of how the course of the 21st century might proceed with a revival of liberal nationalism leading the way. Lind envisions a popular riot in Washington after a conservative Senate blocks a House-backed reform program in the first decade of the 21st century. This catalyzes change over the following 15 years, including the abolition of racial preferences and labels, public financing of elections, rewriting Senate election rules, and instituting a proportional representation electoral system. Along the way numerous special interest tax and subsidy breaks for the rich and business are eliminated, a "single-payer" system of universal higher education is introduced, and sharp new restrictions on most forms of immigration are put into place. A social tariff is introduced, and European-style social market trading blocs replace the corporate race to the bottom, leading to a global rise in living standards. Redistributive policies lead to a flourishing, service sector based middle class. Interestingly, Lind does not mention environmental problems, has little to say about gender norms, and does not mention the potential impact of new technologies in the next century.

Whatever may be the plausibility of this vision, which Lind admits is at best a useful "exercise," his books are also valuable for the critique of contemporary conservatism and the cultural criticism. Regarding conservatives, Lind decries the takeover of "mainstream conservatism" by figures such as Pat Robertson and Pat Buchanan. Buchanan, Lind notes, made the strategic mistake of applying populism consistently, attacking liberal elites and racial minorities as well as corporate elites: Traditional polite Republican strategy relied on only the former as cover for implementing elitist economic policies. Lind also acknowledges that the conservative ideal of yeoman self-reliance does not fit a world of corporate employees; attacking conservative opposition to government entitlements, Lind notes, "If a steady stream of income from a trust fund or shares in a multinational corporation is just as acceptable a basis for republican citizenship as rents from land, then why isn't a steady stream of income from the government to a pensioner or a student? Indeed, if the republic is conceived of as a great corporation, then why shouldn't citizens be regarded as shareholders, with entitlement representing their minimal share of the earnings?" [21]

Finally, Lind is an astute observer of elite culture. In the *Next American Nation* Lind is at his best in providing an accurate and highly entertaining description of the lifestyles and mores of the "white overclass." For instance, Lind notes that

> If you are Episcopalian or Jewish, have a graduate or professional degree from an expensive university, work in a large downtown office building in an East or West Coast metropolis, watch MacNeil/Lehrer on PBS, and are saving for a vacation in London or Paris, you are a card-carrying member of the white overclass, even if your salary is not very impressive. If you are Methodist, Baptist, or Catholic, have a B.A. from a state university, work in or for a small business or for a career government service, watch the Nashville Network on cable, and are saving for a vacation in Las Vegas, Atlantic City, Branson, Missouri, or Orlando, Florida (Disneyworld), you are probably not a member of the white overclass—no matter how much money you make. [22]

Lind, then, has produced some of the most incisive writing in recent years among Beltway pundits, writing that demonstrates substantive appreciation and understanding of both conservative and liberal political traditions, and has passionately made the case for a neo-Trumanesque revival. But Lind's scenarios of a nationalist politics oriented around both opposition to affirmative action and immigration and economic and political populism coming to the fore are not persuasive. If hoping to retake the Democratic Party from corporate control was not difficult enough, Lind's agenda is also likely doomed by the practical fact that attacking affirmative action is a non-starter for building a coalition of liberal voters powerful enough to also enact something like serious campaign reform. The only alternative would be to somehow politicize on moderately liberal lines a large percentage of the population that has little organic connection to the Democratic party or politics in general. In the end, Lind is excessively wedded to a top-down vision of change, as exemplified by his fantasy of a dramatic riot and showdown between cops and citizens in the streets of the nation's capital leading to serious change.

Tony Blair. *New Britain.* Boulder: Westview Press, 1996.

Prior to his election as Prime Minister in April 1997, Tony Blair released a collection of speeches and policy papers spelling out his vision for the Labour government in power. Quite obviously patterned after many of Clinton's 1992 campaign themes, Blair's ideas, as a whole, compare perhaps most directly to Robert Reich's notion of upgrading education and job skills—rather than protecting existing jobs—as the route to economic security in the "new global economy." As has been widely noted, Blair's New Labour has dropped its support for public ownership of industry (outside of transportation and some services) and has explicitly distanced itself from radical trade unions.

Nonetheless, Blair, unlike Clinton, is willing to openly say that his vision is one of social democracy, as spelled out in the notion of a "Stakeholder Britain." Specific pledges by Blair include legislating a minimum wage; promoting industrial cooperation between industry and unions; increasing investments in education and technology, particularly in the knowledge industry; creating a structure for lifelong learning via a "University of Industry" that would provide an ongoing curriculum for adult education; utilizing industrial policy to help small businesses acquire venture capital; upgrading the public transportation system; providing tax rebates for employers who hire the long-term unemployed; improving child care and transport for unemployed persons seeking to move back into the labor market; and numerous other specific initiatives. The overall theme of Blair's program is promoting nationwide cooperation in support of a long-term economic strategy to make Britain a "young, vibrant" economy that can solve its own social problems.

As interesting as Blair's specific positive proposals are the concessions he makes at the outset to the demands of the "global market." "Since it is inconceivable that the UK would want to withdraw unilaterally from this global market-place, we must adjust our policies to its existence," states Blair, noting that capital flows "can swiftly move against policies which fail to win investors' confidence." [23] The upshot is, an expansionary fiscal or monetary policy is simply impossible for the United Kingdom to pursue; indeed Blair cites the notoriously conservative German Bundesbank as a positive model for British monetary policy making. On the fiscal side, Blair endorses the idea of a capital budget to finance borrowing for long-term public investments, noting that cuts in such spending can only damage the "supply side" of the economy. However, Britain must keep all such debts in line with the rest of Europe, and Blair distances himself from "penal taxation." Sounding very much like an American politician, he states that "the objective of any government is to lower rather than to increase the tax burden on ordinary families." [24] Like Clinton, Blair states that changing the composition of the budget is more important than its overall size; by reducing unemployment, Blair hopes to make more funds available for his investment program.

Ultimately, Blair hopes to make Britain a high-skill, high-tech economy with a thriving "knowledge" industry, playing off not least the natural commercial advantages of speaking the English language. All in all, the success of his program should help answer the question of whether a committed social democratic government with fairly modest goals and no hostility to the existing economic order can make any headway towards such progressive goals as reduced inequality and more community, both ideals frequently cited by Blair, in the current global political environment. Compared with Clinton, Blair enjoys the huge advantage of the parliamentary system, and there is little reason to doubt that the vast majority of his program can be implemented over the next five years, more or less as noted in this text. If Clinton was the test case of how well a moderate-liberal program might fare in the post-Cold War American context—not very!—then Blair's government will serve as the best test case for how such a program can fare in a smaller country, with a parliamentary system, and quite possibly a less pliable leader at the helm. However, the initial moves of the Blair administration, such as ending free tuition for all college students, seem to contradict his pro-education platform, and in the early months of his government Blair has taken great pains to avoid lurching the country to the left.

Local-level Economic Alternatives

David L. Imbroscio. *Reconstructing City Politics: Alternative Economic Development and Urban Regimes*. Thousand Oaks, CA: Sage Press, 1997.

This chapter concludes with consideration of four further works on the edge of the mainstream policy discussion that are explicitly aimed not at national level reforms, but at promoting local-level experimentation in community-based economic alternatives. The first work is that of political scientist David Imbroscio. Imbroscio begins his analysis by noting that a range of empirical and theoretical studies by urban regime scholars in the 1980s have produced a consensus that most American cities, most of the time, are governed by pro-growth alliances formed between land-based business interests and elected officials. Because elected officials depend on economic growth and business health to stay in power and for the resources needed to govern effectively, policy tends to be heavily tilted towards business interests. Cities willingly provide subsidies, tax breaks, and zoning assistance to lure outside, mobile corporate capital, and in many cities the tendency is to pour huge amounts of resources into downtown development projects such as sports stadiums and convention centers. These structural patterns reinforce inequality and militate against any agenda oriented towards directing resources to neighborhoods and improving the quality of life of the city's poorer residents. Imbroscio reasons that it is thus necessary for cities to pursue economic development strategies that focus on expanding a city's *own* resources and capacity for self-reliance, not on attracting outside capital. He spells out three possible strategies for doing so.

The first approach available to city policy makers is "entrepreneurial mercantilism." This strategy aims to maximize the flow of resources within the city and to promote the development of locally-owned businesses, while preventing the "leakage" of resources out of the community. Specific policies include technical and financial assistance to local businesses, import substitution policies such as preferences for local firms in city contracts and buyer-supplier networks, energy efficiency and recycling campaigns; city contracts linked to the hiring of local residents; and the creative use of "innovative local finance" tools such as city pension funds and local currencies to support local businesses. Such policies have been implemented on a piecemeal basis in dozens of American cities. Imbroscio explores the reasons why the most comprehensive attempt to date to try to implement a series of policies along these lines, the "Homegrown Economy" (HEP) approach adopted by St. Paul, MN in the 1980s under mayor George Latimer was disappointing in its overall impact: the failure of local business leaders to fully embrace the project; government's incapacity to effectively implement the policies, due partly to the recalcitrance of city bureaucrats; economic factors, such as the high dependence of St. Paul on external resources; and the ultimate withdrawal by Latimer of enthusiasm for the HEP. Still, in Imbrosocio's view the failure of this attempt should not be used to dismiss future use of specific mercantilist policies or the possibility of more successful comprehensive approaches in more favorable settings.

The second set of strategies fall under the label of "community-based economic development." This approach aims to create community-controlled local economic institutions that recycle money within the community and provide for a more egalitarian distribution of wealth and benefits. Ultimately, community-based institutions might provide an alternative concentration of "internal resources" to which local politicians could gravitate in developing policy; stable community-based job-creation capacity would forestall the need for cities to woo outside capital. Cities pursuing this strategy would seek to provide aid and technical assistance to community land trusts, worker-owned firms, community finance institutions, consumer cooperatives, and community development corporations. Attaining effective control of city land would be particularly important in facilitating a community-based strategy.

As with mercantilist approaches, elements of a community-based strategy are surprisingly widespread in American cities, although Pittsburgh, the city Imbroscio identifies as having pursued the most ambitious community-based agenda to date, has failed as yet to significantly impact the structure of local politics by building up community-rooted enterprises.

Imbroscio's third strategy for reconstructing city politics is to develop profit-making city-owned enterprises. Such enterprises can obviously create and anchor jobs locally, and the profit streams from such enterprises can be recycled back into the community (possible in the form of support for community-based or mercantilist policies) or simply help offset the cost of normal government operations (making tax reductions possible). Moreover, Imbroscio notes that while less common than the first two approaches, there are in the United States numerous examples of successful city-owned business in areas such as cable television, hotels, land development, and minor-league baseball. Beyond outright direct ownership, cities might also hold equity in private firms, lease out city-owned land and buildings for private use at public profit, or engage in short-term buying and selling of land at a profit to the public. Imbroscio states that the long-term feasibility of the municipal enterprise is difficult to assess given the relative paucity of empirical evidence.

In the end, Imbroscio is cautious yet optimistic about the capacity of these strategies, used in creative combination with one another, to seriously impact the structures of urban polities in the United States; yet Imbroscio is surely correct in insisting that, logically speaking, the overwhelming tendency of urban regimes to tilt towards business interests in order to help secure outside capital, economic growth and political success can only be plausibly overcome in two ways: by a massive infusion of federal resources to cities, an infusion that is extremely unlikely in the foreseeable future, or by building up alternative resource bases within cities that can be the basis of a different, more inclusive urban regime.

Imbroscio is also correct to say that the current empirical evidence, so far as it goes, invites as much skepticism as hopefulness regarding the possibility of urban reconstruction. Still, there have been many experiments and even a handful of comprehensive efforts even in the absence of major activism and public support for such strategies. The emergence of a serious local-level politics which self-consciously aimed to end the dependence of local cities on outside resources and to build up a community's internal assets might plausibly yield more practical experience—and more success—than is presently visible from the first generation of community economic development efforts in the United States.

Michael Shuman. *Going Local: Creating Self-Reliant Communities in a Global Age*. New York: Free Press, 1998.

Shuman aims to articulate a progressive vision of traditional American entrepreneurialism, rooted in local community. Arguing that the left has spent too much time disparaging corporate America without offering an alternative vehicle for economic development that is plausible within the ideological context of the United States, Shuman forwards the notion of a "community corporation" as an alternative to the primary existing forms of larger-scale business in the United States: privately held and publicly traded corporations, worker-owned firms, nonprofits, and public enterprise. In Shuman's view private corporations are simply not structured to be responsive to the concerns of local communities; worker-owned firms have a mixed record at best; and while public enterprise offers some potential advantages to communities, its efficiency record and susceptibility to corruption make it a dubious institutional form for a progressive entrepreneurialism to embrace.

Shuman argues that a properly structured community corporation can solve many of the problems familiar to the traditional models. The basic idea is that each firm would be rooted in particular geographical communities. The firms would issue two kinds of stock, full voting-rights stock and simple investment stock. Only members of the local community in which the corporation is rooted would be permitted to own voting-rights stock; no individual would be allowed to own more than 1% of any community corporations' voting stock. The stock could be traded, and its investors would be permitted to grow rich. However, highly decentralized decision making among members of a particular community ought to create different motivations and different corporate behavior. Shuman reasons that such an entity would be unlikely to move its operations away from the local community, would be more responsive to the needs of the local community, including its environment, and would recycle a greater share of its profits within the community. Moreover, Shuman believes such corporations would be more likely to create something of functional value for local use, as part of wider self-reliance strategy, than traditional firms which are content to sell to any market in which they can gain a profitable foothold. Shuman cites community credit unions as a successful example of a "community corporation"already widespread in the United States.

While Shuman is favorably inclined towards public enterprise, he argues that Americans are simply not prepared ideologically to accept turning over large chunks of the economy to governmental units, and that public enterprise has a mixed record on the environment and a tendency towards corruption. Against this, it might be argued that local public enterprise in the United States has succeeded even in politically conservative municipalities under the direction of Republican mayors; that the corruptibility of a given public enterprise depends on the openness and accountability of the political culture in which it operates; and that the actual behavior of public entities will often reflect the guiding ideology of its managers, which varies substantially over time and from community to community. It might also appear that public enterprises would be better equipped to handle larger-scale complex manufacturing with numerous inputs and semi-finished goods at multiple production sites, although Shuman proposes Italian-style manufacturing networks to link community corporations together as one way to solve the scale problem.

An additional design problem for the community corporation idea is the possibility that in a given town, the rich and upper-middle class will hold a disproportionate share of the stock and hence have a disproportionate say, as a class, in the town's community corporations. Shuman acknowledges this problem and notes that local organizations, including the town itself, ought to be allowed to hold shares to represent the interests of poorer citizens who cannot afford to invest in stock. (Another possibility for evading this problem is to adopt local-level versions of the Louis Kelso "Stock Ownership for All Plan," in which a local community bank would loan money to medium and low-income individuals for the express purpose of buying stock in community corporations. Dividend payments would then be used to repay the bank [with interest], a process taking perhaps 7-10 years.)

Finally, while the community corporations would indeed be more likely to respond to community concerns, it is not clear why some more successful corporations would not grow over time into large conglomerates that allowed the investors of one community to dominate other communities' firms. A cap on firm size, strict application of antitrust law, or some other mechanism would be needed to contain some community corporations from growing to the point where they are a huge net asset to their base community but a net bad for society as a whole.

While the community corporation idea is critical to Shuman's overall project, he foresees this entity as embedded within a broader set of strategies, institutions, and practices that support local self-reliance and community-building economics. Most critically, Shuman calls on local communities to withdraw government support and subsidies for mobile corporations and instead look for ways to leverage and support start-up community corporations through local subsidies, purchasing and hiring policies, and tax policy. At the national level, Shuman is strongly committed to reversing the emerging free trade regime.

In his final chapter, Shuman spells out a number of additional steps local communities can now take: Drafting a "constitution" of a city's economic aims; publishing an inventory of local needs and resources, in the form of an "audit" or "state of the city" report, on a regular basis, to "shine a light" on the existing local political economy; using that audit to identify promising areas for new community corporations; training "progressive entrepreneurs"; starting community banks and local currencies; and finally, connecting the takeover of city hall to national and international politics through municipal lobbying of the federal government and through problem-solving partnerships on particular issues between sister cities in different countries. (One example of the latter cited by Shuman is the Climate Alliance, which consists of over 150 European cities that have committed to substantial cuts in greenhouse gas emission by the year 2010 while also providing assistance to indigenous peoples' efforts to protect the Brazilian rainforests.) Shuman believes that with the new information technology, the opportunity now exists to develop a localist orientation to political and economic reconstruction that leads not to isolation but to real sharing of information and ideas on a national and international basis.

Ultimately, Shuman declares that "The great struggle of the 21st century will be between those who believe in cheap goods and those who believe in place." [25] Although Shuman is probably too sanguine in stating that developing new community corporations that return profits to communities and behave in a responsible way will cause existing corporations to "either adapt or die," his thorough description of the community corporation concept is a valuable contribution to the policy toolbox of those who indeed "believe in place."

Susan Meeker-Lowry. *Invested in the Common Good*. Philadelphia: New Society Publishers, 1995.

Vermont activist Meeker-Lowry in this volume provides impressive documentation of on-the-ground efforts to "do" alternative, community-sustaining economics in North America. The result is a fine primer on the who, what, why, and how of some of the most successful experimentation now underway. After a brief introductory section in which Meeker-Lowry sketches her own philosophy for an "earth-centered" economic praxis, the book goes on to describe different kinds of community-based institutions, followed by profiles of specific success stories. Among the institutions covered are socially responsible investment vehicles, community development banks and credit unions, revolving loan funds, alternative currencies, community land trusts, community-supported agriculture, and contemporary Native American efforts in self-sufficient economic development. Meeker-Lowry does not cover either worker-owned firms or locally-scaled public enterprise in her book; nor is there any attempt to specify how this array of community-rooted institutions might add up to larger-scale social and economic change. Rather, the intent here is to convey a "sense of magic and inspirations with the practical how-tos" in the spirit of helping a thousand flowers to bloom, in the genuine hope that the different pieces can add up to a coherent "picture" of the future.[26]

Barbara Brandt. *Whole Life Economics: Revaluing Daily Life* Philadelphia, PA : New Society Publishers, 1995.

Brandt provides a critique of "old paradigm" economics that aims at profit maximization to the exclusion of other social goals, and which renders invisible many other forms of economic activity, such as unpaid work done in the home and elsewhere. Like the Meeker-Lowry volume, this book provides a basic overview of on-the-ground local-level economic alternatives that embody what Brandt calls "new paradigm" economics, and are aimed at meeting human needs in a holistic sense. (As with the Meeker-Lowry book, discussion of local-level public enterprise is notably absent.)

Brandt argues that the notion of holistic natural systems (as provided by recent work in the sciences) should inform a vision of a non-hierarchical, community-embracing paradigm for economic life. Brandt is particularly convincing in her rejection of Abraham Maslow's "hierarchy of needs" schema, noting that the traditional pyramid notion of needs can lead to absurd conclusions: that poor people have no meaningful spiritual life or experiences of self-actualization, or that economically developed societies are the happiest and most fulfilled. Brandt proposes an alternative set of "needs" which should be equally valued: "survival needs," "needs for care," "needs for amenities," "occasional needs for luxuries," and "need to replenish the sources that support and sustain us." [27]

While the thrust of Brandt's book is admirable, it also points to the limitation of a purely bottom-up approach. Brandt puts forward no strategic vision of how the various alternatives she cites could ever fundamentally challenge the ongoing power structure of corporate capitalism, nor does she take up the question occupying most of the bibliography's next chapter: What does a coherent, functional system based on values like those espoused by Brandt look like? Brandt is particularly suspect in her discussion of corporations and socially responsible business: "In order to place businesses in a more healthy relationship with the rest of life, we need to allow them to give up their privileged position in society and not require them to pursue addictive goals such as constant growth and constantly rising profits." [28]

According to Brandt's analysis, actors in the current system are motivated essentially by greed and addiction to more, including corporations. While re-chartering corporations and requiring citizen participation in corporate decisions would be helpful, Brandt implies that measures such as changing legal codes to allow corporations to give more profits away or allowing corporations that have "fulfilled their mission" to close down would somehow lead to a serious change in corporate behavior. This assumes that corporations 1) have an interest in actually changing their behavior and 2) could substantially change such behavior if they wanted to, on a voluntary basis, while still operating in a competitive market where other actors are always lining up to take away one company's market share. Both assumptions are extremely implausible as generalizations, even if true in some specific cases.

While bottom-up, locally rooted alternatives can play a leading role in a coherent, practical vision of the future, the problem of the large corporation—and just what the basic economic unit of a good society should be—must be faced up to in an honest way that does not evade the power realities: Corporations function to convert workers' effort into profits for shareholders, and have a strong interest in preserving their own status and prerogatives, not simply because of "greed," but out of fear of losing market share and declining. While it is not inconceivable that a handful of American corporations might be influenced to some degree by parts of Brandt's "new paradigm," the larger, much more difficult reality cannot be wished away.

Additional References

Amitai Etzioni. *The New Golden Rule*. New York: Basic Books, 1996.

Amitai Etzioni. T*he Spirit of Community*. New York: Crown Publishers, 1993.

Peter Brown. *Restoring the Public Trust: A Fresh Vision for Progressive Government in America*. Boston: Beacon Press, 1994.

Robert Frank and Philip Cook. *The Winner-Take-All Society*. New York: The Free Press, 1995.

Robert Heilbroner. *Visions of the Future*. New York: W.W. Norton and Company, 1995.

Robert Helibroner. *21st Century Capitalism*. New York: W.W. Norton and Company, 1993.

Paul Kennedy. *Preparing for the 21st Century*. New York: Random House, 1993.

James Carville. *We're Right, They're Wrong: A Handbook for Spirited Progressives*. New York: Random House, 1996.

Immanuel Wallerstein. *After Liberalism*. New York: The New Press, 1995.

Christopher Lasch. *The Revolt of the Elites*. New York: W.W. Norton and Company, 1995.

Christopher Lasch. *The True and Only Heaven*. New York: W.W. Norton and Company, 1991.

William Greider. *Who Will Tell the People*. New York: Simon and Schuster, 1992.

Benjamin Barber. *Jihad vs. McWorld*. New York: Random House, 1995.

Samuel Bowles and Herbert Gintis. *Democracy and Capitalism: Property, Community, and the Contradictions of Modern Social Thought*. New York: Basic Books, 1986.

Theda Skocpol and Stanley Greenberg, eds. *The New Majority*. New Haven: Yale University Press, 1997.

Stephanie Coontz. *The Way We Really Are: Coming to Terms With America's Changing Families*. New York: Basic Books, 1997.

Richard Barnet and John Cavanagh. *Global Dreams: Imperial Corporations and the New World Order*. New York: Simon and Schuster, 1994.

Marcus Raskin and Chester Hartman, eds. *Winning America: Ideas and Leadership for the 1990s*. Boston: South End Press/Washington: Institute for Policy Studies, 1988.

Robert McElvaine. *What's Left?: A New Democratic Vision for America.* Holbrook, MA: Adams Media Corporation, 1996.

Mickey Kaus. *The End of Equality.* New York: Basic Books, 1991.

Wallace Peterson. *Silent Depression: The Fate of the American Dream.* New York: W.W. Norton, 1994.

Bennett Harrison. *Lean and Mean: The Changing Landscape of Corporate Power in an Age of Flexibility.* New York: Basic Books, 1994.

Jim Hightower. *There's Nothing in The Middle of the Road But Yellow Stripes and Dead Amarillos.* New York: HarperCollins, 1997.

Lisbeth B. Schorr. *Common Purpose: Strengthening Families and Neighborhoods to Rebuild America.* New York: Anchor Books, 1997.

Jeffrey Madrick. *The End of Affluence.* New York: Random House, 1995.

Chapter Two

Market Socialism and Related Proposals

Introduction and Overview

The most fertile terrain in the past decade for detailed discussion of a what an alternative social system might look like has been amongst a growing number of academic economists who have attempted to specify and defend proposals for a "market socialist" economy.

Major writers in the field to date include British economists Alec Nove, David Miller, Saul Estrin, and Pat Devine, each of whom has presented distinct visions of a post-capitalist economy; and the American economists Leland Stauber, Thomas Weisskopf, David Schweickart, James Yunker, John Roemer (often in collaboration with Pranab Bardhan), and Robin Hahnel (in collaboration with left journalist Michael Albert).

Writers on both sides of the Atlantic owe significant debts to notions of "reform socialism," "market socialism," and "socialism with a human face" generated by reformist economists and politicians in Eastern Europe, starting with Czechoslovakia in the 1960s and continuing in the efforts at worker self-management in Yugoslavia in the 1970s. Many of these economists including Sik, Brus, Liska, and Tardos, have continued to express views and models regarding "market socialism" into the 1980s and 90s.

The maturity of the contemporary market socialist debate is best evidenced by the numerous literature reviews and assessments of existing proposals offered by both British and American writers in recent years. A 1992-93 issue of the *Review of Radical Political Economy* devoted to market socialism, for instance, contained fruitful dialogue between advocates of mixed-economy market socialism and full-blown participatory planners Michael Albert and Robin Hahnel, as well as numerous other contributions from key figures in the debate.

In 1994, an American professor at the University of Alabama-Birmingham, N. Scott Arnold, published a critical assessment of existing market socialist proposals; Arnold took issue with both the technicalities of the proposals and the claim that such changes would in fact significantly realize "socialist" or "progressive" values if implemented. Also in 1994, while serving as Council of Economic Advisers chair, Joseph Stiglitz published *Whither Socialism?*, which expresses the important view that market socialist notions would in fact be viable if markets themselves conformed to neoclassical models, but that since in the real world neoclassical expectations (particularly regarding information) are almost never present, the theoretical basis for market socialism is defunct. (Stiglitz's critique is aimed more at the older market socialist literature generated from the 1930s work of Oskar Lange than at current proposals.) Stiglitz nonetheless allows that an extensive role for the state, including public enterprise, is still appropriate, and notes the surprising success of the peculiar property regime evident in the contemporary Chinese economy (including, in addition to a growing number of outright entrepreneurs, a mix of cooperatives, local-level public enterprises, and larger-scale state enterprises in which property rights are often ambiguous).

Probably the most important discussion of the literature to date, however, is that found in University of Stirling political scientist Christopher Pierson's *Socialism after Communism: The New Market Socialism*. Pierson skillfully analyzes the range of existing proposals and then subjects the market socialist view—best summarized as "social ownership" of capital plus markets—to critiques from both left and right (with particular emphasis on the views of F.A. Hayek).

Pierson concludes that claims of market socialism's economic viability are on the whole "contested but defensible," but notes that almost no theorist has yet even attempted to lay out a plausible political theory of transition to such an economy from within advanced capitalism. Pierson adds that, as a species of "electoral socialism," the proposals, even if adopted by progressive political parties as a central strategy, will face the same political problems as all versions of "electoral socialism," (as best laid out by Adam Przeworski in the mid-1980s). Consequently, Pierson himself is skeptical but not dismissive of "market socialism" as a viable strategy for "left-center" political forces in advanced capitalist societies.

The following bibliography contains descriptions in some detail of the positions of most of the thinkers noted above, as well as the relevant references. However, it is useful to lay out at the outset a general summary of some of the obvious characteristics (and omissions) of the various brands of market socialism.

1. Market socialists generally are attempting to sketch a society in which capitalist accumulation of wealth is replaced by "social"—that is, public—ownership of the bulk of the productive capital in society, with the market retained as an instrument of organizing production, distribution and consumption . The primary deviations from this position come from British writers Pat Devine and Michael Barratt Brown, the team of Michael Albert and Robin Hahnel, and traditional Marxist David McNally, all of whom reject markets.

2. As Pierson notes, market socialists in general accept the neoclassical claim of superior efficiency for the market, and generally underemphasize traditional left, pro-planning arguments regarding the tremendous waste evident under capitalism (in the form of underutilized productive factors, socially perverse incentives generated by private enterprise, community instability, and the costs of thrown-away cities, etc).

3. Market socialist thinkers to date offer no systematic effort to contend with the ecological issues raised by Herman Daly and other ecological economists regarding the need for a steady-state economy. A few, most convincingly David Schweickart, have tried to demonstrate that a market socialist economy would at least improve upon capitalism's ecological record.

4. Most market socialists reject the notion of changing human nature or transforming market culture in general; there is no attempt to alter the set of human aspirations markets generate, and even the goal of sharply reduced income inequalities is not a given in the literature. Most contemporary market socialists do not claim their proposals will lead to an egalitarian society, but at best to a modestly more just society where those at the bottom are not totally excluded from the fruits of the economy. Any notion of generating a different sense of self or aspirations (as called for by those in the anti-consumerism movement) is simply not a part of these schemes and is viewed with considerable scorn in many instances. The traditional socialist notion of building a society based on expanded cooperation and a sense of common purpose, while not entirely abandoned, is also not a central consideration for those theorists who accept the primacy of markets.

5. There is a sharp divide in the literature between those who advocate worker self-management--most notably David Miller and David Schweickart—as the core institution in a market socialist economy, and those who foresee little change in corporate management relations, other than profits being returned to the public.

6. Opinion ranges widely among market socialists as to the role of the state; the locus of control over the economy (local public ownership vs. national institutions, etc.); the nature of macroeconomic governance; and how much and what type of planning will be carried out. While all market socialists claim (or hope) that their proposals will subject economic decision making to significant democratic control and reduce the distortions on political democracy generated by capitalism, there is considerable variation among thinkers as to how to do it.

7. Most market socialists spend little time justifying their positions on appeal to political values (socialist, democratic, or otherwise) and take as *a priori* the moral imperative to move beyond capitalism. Important and useful exceptions are Miller and especially Schweickart, who explicitly frames his proposals in terms of democracy, liberty, equality, and autonomy, and attempts to engage (without always validating) the position of serious conservatives (Hayek, Friedman). Schweickart is also the only thinker to (explicitly) extend his vision of market socialism to a consideration of global consequences; he argues that a market socialist regime would seriously undercut traditional pressures towards imperialistic foreign policy under advanced capitalism, especially in the United States.

8. As Pierson notes, no market socialist theorist has yet articulated a plausible theory of political transition to such a society from within advanced capitalism, although, to be fair, some proponents, such as Roemer, explicitly state that there may be more favorable political climates for their proposals in the formerly socialist or developing worlds.

Basic Models of Market Socialism

Leland Stauber. "A Proposal for a Democratic Market Economy," *Journal of Comparative Economics,* 1977, Vol.1 No.3. Reprinted in *A New Program for Democratic Socialism: Lessons from Austria.* Carbondale, Ill: Four Willows Press, 1987.

Stauber's proposed version of market socialism contains three sectors:

1) Government operations, including nationalized industries where uniquely appropriate, municipal utilities, etc;
2) A corporate sector with ownership held by a network of local government banks;
3) Privately owned small businesses.

Stauber states that "The proposed conception is neutral with respect to decision on the optimum mix of market forces and government economic planning or other government intervention." However, "The political experience of such use of national governmental power to remove large individual and family wealth would work pervasive changes in public attitudes in the United States (even in the attitudes of business executives) toward government power and activity itself and hence toward the use of government for other social purposes in a vast number of fields of public policy... The result would be pervasive shifts in the content of American public policies." [29]

Governments can thus regulate or subsidize at will, as in contemporary mixed economies. However, the heart of the proposal, the publicly owned, corporate-organized sector, is to be made efficient by participating in the market, free from governmental operative control. These firms can fail; their goal is to attract credit from local government-owned banks by paying out the highest possible profit. Discipline would be obtained much as under the current system—shareholders, public, not private, sit on the boards of firms and hire and fire managers based on their capacity to maximize profits. A hierarchical system of firm organization is envisioned.

Each local public investment bank would seek to maximize returns to their communities through wise investments in a range of corporate enterprises; no investment bank could own more than 7% of any given enterprise. Local investment banks would also be banned from investing in enterprises in their own geographic area (or conspiring with other governments to trade investment funds into each other's localities).

Under Stauber's plan,

> ...the socialization of existing business corporations would signify only changes in the holdings of corporate securities. The firms themselves would retain the corporate identity, internal governance in the legal rights of management and stockholders, and the legal status provided under the general incorporation laws. Private promoters would act in an entirely private capacity and have complete freedom of enterprise, but they would be required for any venture requiring the corporate form, given whatever leveling of private wealth had been brought about by taxation, to seek their capital from the proposed capital market in publicly owned investment funds. In doing so they would have to make their case for the profitability of their venture in a manner differing in no essential way whatever from existing business practice.[30]

Stauber argues that stockholder control over management would be more effective than under existing capitalism because stockholder power would be far less fragmented, consisting of 15-20 professional investment managers representing localities. As with the "Capitalism for All" plan offered by Louis Kelso in the 1950s and 60s, Stauber would change corporate financing laws so that 90% of all dividends would have to be paid out and all new capital would have to be attained via the local investment fund mechanism. This would also up the ante on efficiency: questionable projects within a big corporation could not be funded from the corporation's internal profits but would require external financing in competition with smaller firms.

Land would be socially owned and leased out by the public to private users on a long-term basis.

This is an ingenious proposal in many ways. It does not deal with the environmental/"public bad" issue at all, nor planning for community economic stability over time; but it assumes that life in this society would change the political assumptions about government's role and therefore facilitate strong social democratic policies. Stauber cites as evidence the attitudes of Western European business executives towards public enterprise and government. Living in systems where government intervention is accepted, they exhibit none of the hostilities to government U.S. CEOs generally evince. (Stauber, in an unpublished manuscript focusing on land ownership, convincingly spells out the cultural/ideological consequences of different ownership regimes. For instance, in Swedish communities with a long history of community land, land is viewed as inviolably belonging to the community, not a private commodity.) This evidence is central to Stauber's explanation of why his economy would attain capitalist-like efficiencies: After becoming accustomed to working for the government, managers would be just as motivated as when working for private masters; and even if the top echelon quit in ideological protest to socialism, the next rank would happily take its place.

Stauber comes down on the conservative side on the question of labor motivation, seeing unemployment, bankruptcy threats, and hierarchy—the market—as key guarantors of discipline. Those coming down on the opposite side see job security, participation in management, and profit-related incentives as generating ample motivation to maintain high productivity.

David Miller

"A Vision of Market Socialism," *Dissent*, Summer 1991.
Market, State, and Community, Oxford: Clarendon Press, 1990.

Miller's model is representative of a "worker-owned" socialist model. In Miller's conception, the entire economy is to be organized into fairly small-scale, worker-owned factories of 500 employees or less, which he thinks not unrealistic from a technical point of view. Miller cites studies showing that it is difficult for cooperatives to maintain democratic practices and succeed economically when they grow past 500 workers.

From an organizational point of view, this is a leap back to small-scale capitalism. The efficiencies of the multiplant firm which allocates its resource on a managerial basis instead of using the market—economies of scale—are foregone, as Miller explicitly acknowledges. However, the small size of firms will also eliminate efficiencies associated with oligopolistic control of markets in capitalist economies, offsetting the efficiency loss from sticking with a smaller-sized industrial organization.

Each firm is to be organized on a democratic basis and can only expand by giving new workers full democratic rights and profit stakes. (As critic Frank Roosevelt points out, this is likely to lead to capital-intensive organization of production to maximize profits per worker and may therefore threaten overall full employment.)

Miller rejects centralized economic planning but endorses welfare state and regulatory measures along strong social democratic lines, including the provision of a minimum income (but not a universal social wage). The source of micro-efficiency is simply threat of business failure, as now, along with profit-sharing. He does not specify whether the state will guarantee full employment or not, or whether this would have any effect on internal discipline. In other words, how costly to the individual worker would becoming unemployed really be?

Financing for the worker firms would come from outside each enterprise, possibly from a plurality of public investment banks charged with balancing economic and social criteria in allotting capital. These banks would be subject to periodic review by elected bodies. (Clearly, Miller and Stauber's models might be made to fit together: worker-owned firms financed by investment banks owned by local governments. The only question would be to whom the profits would go, the workers or the governments. Conceivably it could be 50-50.)

Finally, Miller gives three reasons why a worker-owned enterprise might be expected to be environmentally sounder than traditional capitalist enterprise:

First, since profits are shared, the economic benefit for any one individual of polluting the community is lowered.

Second, "The effects of environmental pollution will also be felt more widely among those responsible for making the decisions," that is, workers who handle toxic wastes will try to minimize the incidence of such waste.

Third, key managerial decisions will be more open and harder to hide.

These observations are interesting, and probably correct so far as they go, but not convincing on the larger question of whether a worker economy would be inherently sustainable ecologically (particularly in light of the more stringent ecological criteria forwarded by Herman Daly and others). The familiar dynamic of conflict between producers and community (the "externalities" problem) still remains, and economic growth itself would still likely generate increased ecological pressure under a functional Miller-type economy.

John Roemer

Pranab Bardhan and John E. Roemer, "Market Socialism: A Case for Rejuvenation," *Journal of Economic Perspectives*, Vol.6, No.3, Summer 1992.

John E. Roemer, "Market Socialism: A Blueprint," *Dissent*, Fall 1991.

John E. Roemer, *A Future for Socialism*. Cambridge: Harvard University Press, 1994.

John E. Roemer and contributors, *Equal Shares*. New York: Verso Books, 1996.

Roemer's vision of market socialism, as laid out in two distinct but complementary proposals, has three unique merits:

First, Roemer offers a detailed discussion of the "agency" or "soft budget constraint" problem under market socialism—how enterprises are to be held financially accountable under public ownership—and a *keiretsu*-like proposal to get out of it;

Second, he provides a theoretical argument about why market socialism would produce less "public bads;"

Thirdly, Roemer fruitfully discusses different ways investment planning could work under market socialism.

To take up each in turn, in greater detail:

Agency

Roemer notes that with the separation of ownership and management, the current corporate capitalist system has considerable agency costs as well, as manifested by high CEO salaries. Supposedly, today's managers are to be disciplined by the managerial labor market, which could easily be reproduced under a Roemer-like market socialism, and the capital market, which would not exist under market socialism. Roemer suggests that the threat of corporate take-over (in the capital market) has proven to be less efficient than a *keiretsu* like arrangement, as in Japan and Germany, where firms are organized around banks which in turn have a strong say in each firm's operations.

Thus, under Roemer's first proposal (originally developed by Roemer's colleague and occasional co-author, Pranab Bardhan), publicly owned firms under private day-to-day control would be organized in groupings around a modest number of state-owned central banks. While under private control, workers would have the right to elect their own managers. A given firm would have multiple shareholders: its own workers, other public firms in its corporate grouping, the main bank in its grouping, outside institutional investors (such as pension funds or educational institutions), local governments, and outside banks.

All borrowing comes from the main bank. With each firm in a group having a share in every other firm, there would be joint monitoring. Ideally each corporate grouping would be in related lines to foster knowledgeable cross-monitoring and sharing of technological innovations among the firms. The bank is the main monitor, however, communicating information about each firm to all other firms, and taking control when profits fall—that is, firing management or restructuring the firm (presumably, in some cases, eliminating plants and workers and communities.) According to Bardhan and Roemer, "The main bank is motivated to arrange the rescue operation, a disproportionate share of which cost is borne by the bank, by its desire to retain its reputation of credibility as a delegated monitor, in a system of reciprocal delegated monitoring with a small number of other main banks. It also does not want to lose the intangible asset it has accumulated specific to its relationship with the affiliate firm." [31] But if it has to sell off a bankrupt firm, it will.

A legitimate question is, who monitors the banks under this system? Roemer's answer hinges more on prestige than material interest: "The key is that these public banks will be in competition to represent, or to induct into their industrial groups, successful firms (including new firms). Thus, a bank wants to build a reputation as a sound financial manager, one that maintains profitability in its group." [32] Likewise, "The reputational concerns of the main bank's managers may act as an antidote to susceptibility to political pressures. The managerial labor market may not 'forget' if a bank manager forgives bad loans or non-performing loans too often." [33]

At first glance, this answer seems to be projecting a feature of capitalist *keiretsus* onto a socialist system. This appeal to the concerns of bankers for protecting their own reputations seems to imply an anti-democratic culture of bureaucratic striving for power at the heart of these banks. But Roemer also suggests that bank manager salaries could be pegged to performance, and that international competition, allowing private institutional investors to hold shares in banks, and safeguards against excessive state intervention in the banks' operation could all help provide the needed context of discipline.

Socialized profit streams run on three tiers in this system: 1) to worker-shareholders within each group, who would own shares not only in their own firm but in all the other firms in the group, 2) to local government investors and 3) to the state itself, which then redistributes total leftover profits in the form of a nationwide social dividend, or spends it on public services. But there also would be "private" profit streams running to nonprofit institutional investors and other publicly-owned firms.

Roemer's second scheme is also interesting in terms of agency. Essentially, profits of all major firms would be socialized and organized into various mutual funds, with each citizen getting a share in a fund. Citizens could move their shares ("clamshells") from less profitable to more profitable mutual funds, but could at no point sell out to the rich for money. Mutual fund managers would then invest or disinvest in firms according to their profitability, and when a given firm's clamshell price goes down, banks would know that a firm is in trouble, and would apply discipline. (The clamshells are not equity, but symbolic shares of property rights.) Roemer estimates that implementing this system would provide each American adult with an annual social dividend of roughly $1,000 (and possibly much more, given the recent stock market boom). This dividend would have a drastic, positive impact on the distribution of income, both by giving a substantial boost to those at the bottom and by reducing the capital income of the richest Americans.

In this model, as with corporate capitalism, capital markets (the banks operating on price signals offered by mutual funds' clamshell movements) and the managerial market are assumed to suffice for attaining discipline and profit-seeking. The same strategy for monitoring the banks noted above holds. Still we might ask—as would conservatives who say that the supposed separation of ownership and management under corporate capitalism is exaggerated, or radicals who think that "working for someone else" dampens productivity—would anyone in the firm benefit personally from the firm's profit-seeking if it's all socialized? (We might also ask this of Stauber's firms). If not, wouldn't this lead to an entire economy of worker/firms settling for middling efficiency, a massive free rider problem that results in macro-level stagnation? Or would there be some percentage of worker/private ownership of shares? In other words, all the discipline for the individual firm seems to come from above in this system and is, in fact, negative discipline. (Unemployment and bankruptcy threats would also be used, apparently.)

Even if it worked, as several left-wing critics have argued , Roemer's scheme might not be socially desirable, since it does maintain conglomerated corporate power and would probably perpetuate a culture of fear and hierarchy in the work place. Within the logic of the market, adjusting Roemer's second model to allow, say, a firm's workers the unequivocal rights to 40 or 50% of its profits, with the rest socialized, might lead to a more efficient dynamic, but generate more inequality. (These same concerns apply to the first Roemer model, where profit is only semi-socialized.)

The political economy of "public bads" under market socialism.

Roemer has developed more fully the same point made by David Miller. Under capitalism a small percentage of persons own a huge amount of stock, so their private gain from, say, polluting, is far higher than their share of the public bad, pollution. Under market socialism, any one person's increase in welfare from higher profits generated by unsound ecological activity is far less likely to outweigh their share of the public bad, since no once person has a huge claim on profits.

This seems unassailable logically, but not sufficient on ecological grounds unless we assume that public bads are dispersed equally across geography and class. I may experience none of the public harm generated when the company my clamshells are invested in dumps toxic wastes on poor African-Americans in Alabama, and would vote for it to get the extra $25 in social dividend. In other words, there's no serious answer to the environmental "system problem" that allows people in one place to sanction polluting someone elsewhere; virtually by definition a systemic solution to pollution must give people control over the toxins generated in the communities where they live.

Investment planning

"The principal point of my discussion of investment planning is that it is possible for the government to redress the market failures involving investment without direct administrative allocation of investment goods..." [34]

Roemer has stated that if market socialism had no capacity to plan investments, it would lose its political rationale vis-a-vis social democracy. Roemer has modeled the relative effectiveness of:

1) central commands to firms
2) direct investment by government
3) adjusting sectoral interest rates
4) adjusting sales taxes on various goods to direct investment in a market socialist regime.

Roemer concludes that a system of pegging interest rates for different sectors at different levels would probably be the most efficacious planning mechanism. Critics have charged that this would lead to a new broker state as lobbyists representing industries clamored to be pegged at low rates. (Similar criticism has been directed at all industrial policy, but under Roemer's scheme the lobbyists would only represent bureaucrats, not well-financed capital.) Although Roemer does make a comment about directing investment to particular geographic areas, the interest rate paradigm of planning does not assure community full employment. But it is reasonable to believe that "indicative planning" could indeed be an excellent tool for allocating capital in a new system that takes into account an assessment of the nation's or region's needs and goals: Such planning might result in, say, 1% interest charges for solar panel producers and 15% interest charges for auto producers, and so forth.

James Yunker. *Socialism Revised and Modernized*. New York: Praeger Press, 1992.

Yunker proposes a market socialism in which ownership rights of corporations would be transferred to a Bureau of Public Ownership (BPO), conceived as an entity of the Federal Government. This BPO would pay a social dividend, and then employ teams of monitors to make sure the still privately controlled corporations were out there making money. CEOs would maintain their positions and be paid based on their performance. BPO "agents" (about 4,000 Yunker estimates) would serve one seven-year term and have their pay largely tied to a "small percentage of the property return generated by the corporations within his or her responsibility." (Imagine the status that job would have! Better than a senator). Note that this is again an attempt to configure a discipline system based on fear in a socialist mode.

Bankruptcy, market competition, and capital market competition are the other spurs to efficiency under Yunker's proposal, which he explicitly cites as being exactly the same tools found in corporate capitalism. All the other features of capitalism also remain, including the private banking system (under BPO oversight); Yunker does, however, propose two government-run investment banks as well.

Tibor Liska. As noted in Lane Kenworthy, "What Kind of Economic System: A Leftist's Guide," *Socialist Review*, 1990, #2, pp. 102-124. See also J. Barsony, "Tibor Liska's Concept of Socialist Entrepreneurship" in *Aecta Oeconomica*, Vol.28, No.3-4 (1982).

Liska, a Hungarian economist, proposes that publicly owned enterprises be auctioned off to entrepreneurs promising the highest rate of profit return to the state, to be paid as an "enterprise use tax." Profits above those bid to the state go to the entrepreneur; however, the entrepreneur can be outbid and lose enterprise control at any time, so as profits increase, the incentive will be to raise one's own bid continually so as to maintain enterprise control. In addition to the enterprise use tax, collateral is paid up front in the case of enterprise failure and bankruptcy. The state would have a minimal role, not even welfare state functions, but would run the auction and distribute a "social inheritance," for example, a social wage, funded by profits and taxes. This social wage would help a person buy their education, and also give everyone the resources to bid on an enterprise and become an entrepreneur. (For really huge enterprises, perhaps there could be collective bids at the auctions.) Those who don't bid could conceivably choose not to work and live off of their social wage.

Obviously, this system has little to say about democratic decision making in the work place or ecological considerations. But the economics of this proposal seems plausible as one element of a new system, particularly in the case of small businesses (of 10-50 employees) that do not choose to be coops. One precursor along these lines is the current practice of government leases to vendors at national parks, airports, and so forth, which guarantee government a revenue stream while entrepreneurs accept the risk.

Marton Tardos. As noted in Kenworthy, "What Kind of Economic System: A Leftist's Guide," *Socialist Review*, 1990, #2, pp. 102-124; Tardos, "Development Program for Economic Control and Organization in Hungary," *Aecta Oeconomica*, Vol. 28, No.3-4 (1982).

Hungarian economist Marton Tardos's idea is to set up holding companies, autonomous from the state, that administer a cluster of firms. The cluster would work in a manner similar to Roemer's proposal, with all financing for firms (save internal profits) coming from the holding company. The holding company runs the show, including choosing whether or not to impose hard budget constraints on each firm and when and where to reallocate new investment. The holding companies have hard budget constraints themselves and must compete for financing from a network of state-owned banks. Holding companies are not allowed to lose money—they go bankrupt. The heads of holding companies and the banks are political appointees, so efficient management of the economy becomes a major political imperative for the party in power. What is socialist about this proposal is that the banks' profits eventually remit to the state.

Beyond the new ownership structure, nothing else about capitalism would change under Tardos's system.

Market Socialism with Explicit Democratic Planning

David Schweickart

"Socialism, Democracy, Market, Planning: Putting the Pieces Together."
Review of Radical Political Economics, Fall-Winter 1992.
Against Capitalism. Cambridge: Cambridge University Press, 1993.

Schweickart appears to have the most fully developed market socialist model, and the model most attuned to the goal of community economic stability. Schweickart is also unusually meticulous in defending the philosophical and economic bases of his proposal, and in my judgment his work sets the standard for comprehensive alternative proposals published to date. However, his proposal itself may not be seen as perfect by all.

The basic structure consists of socially owned, worker-controlled firms in a competitive market. Each firm pays a user tax on capital (keeping profits above this user tax for its own ends or wage bonuses). This user tax funds new investment, accounting for as much as 15% of the GDP, in the economy; new investment is to be planned. The size of the user tax is the principal method of national macroeconomic planning. (A little reflection leads one to think that actual year-to-year changes in this tax would necessarily be tiny so as to prevent great imbalances in outcomes; in other words, Schweickart presupposes great skill in macro-management at the national level.)

How this structure works: A national public capital program is planned and allocated for roads, rail, etc. Routine public administration costs, however, are paid out of other sets of taxes. Also, public investments pay no user taxes. Priorities for "private" investment are recommended and reflected in differential capital user tax rates. What is left over from the federal level is passed on a per capita basis to the states. States pass their public investment programs and may add further conditions on how "private investment" should be prioritized by adding their own modifications to user tax rates. What is left over from that is passed on a per capita basis to local-level community capital banks.

It is these community banks which allocate new investment to firms, acting in a foundation-like manner by evaluating various grant proposals on a strictly bottom-line basis. Bank managers' pay and jobs are tied directly to performance. Each bank would also have a special division to identify emerging entrepreneurial opportunities and award grants to make such ideas go. There would be strong incentive to make this operation effective, since unused community capital is returned to the national level annually. (Wouldn't this enhance the likelihood of throwing money at bad projects to keep the money local? Why not allow communities to save for projected long-term projects?) This system of using local banks to allocate capital would be the most important mechanism of planning for community full employment.

Finally, should local investment allocations lead to unbalanced development—too many book publishers, not enough ditch diggers—not only would the market drive some of the publishers under, but the state authority could take corrective measures based on its continual monitoring of investment decisions. Moreover, all the local banks would have access to such information, so imbalances could be identified early. Even so, this could be a very costly process of correction.

What happens to firms that can't pay the user tax? The worker firm is dissolved, and the capital returns to the public, where it is applied to another enterprise.

Schweickart also takes a different approach to equality. Obviously there are unsocialized profits (surpluses beyond the required user tax payments) in this proposed economy—which are presumably spurs to microefficiency, along with increased participation and less alienation—and Schweickart does not propose a universal social dividend. He instead proposes a formal, legal abolition of wage labor, except perhaps in tiny firms involving a small handful of people. All others must be organized as worker cooperatives.

This is a noble proposition, but it creates one serious worry: if all but the tiniest firms must depend on banks for new investment, won't that slow down the economy and entrepreneurship in general, unless we assume that the bank bureaucracies (which would have to be quite massive) can respond to a small firm's capital request as quickly as a present-day commercial bank?

This seems possible, but would require that the public banks' case-by-case decisions be at least as arbitrary and luck-oriented as current banks' decisions. This condition thereby undercuts Schweickart's claim to "rational"planning, at least at the micro-level. Schweickart does leave the door open to some form of worker/citizen ownership rights on a partial basis, which would allow for independent financing. Theoretically, untaxed profits could be accumulated within the firm to finance self-expansion, but we can assume most workers would prefer to see their unsocialized profits in higher wages and wait for public investment money to come through.

The other problem with abolishing wage labor is how to organize workers within public administration. Who would want a worker-run Los Angeles Police Department?

In terms of maintaining liberty—which requires that citizens have an effective power and economic base outside state mechanisms, in the classic conservative formulation—one may question the wisdom of placing *all* new investment powers in state mechanisms. Still, Schweickart's scheme could easily be revised in a non-totalist direction, and his proposals for administering investments at various levels of authority are valuable.

Regarding ecological issues, Schweickart is correct to insist that his model would likely do better than capitalism, and he is unusual among market socialist proponents in his extended treatment of the sustainability problem. The force of his argument, however, rests on four claims, two of them tenuous. First, Schweickart correctly states that the lack of capital mobility in his model will greatly enhance the possibility for local and regional level regulation of firms within the market, since companies can no longer threaten to move, and the guarantee of capital funds to each region on a per capita basis ends the threat of capital strike. Second, Schweickart plausibly claims that since the public ultimately controls all public disbursements of capital, directing capital towards needed major investments in ecological improvement, be it reforestation or home weatherization, ought to be easier than under capitalism.

Third, Schweickart argues that worker-owned firms are inherently sensitive to the environment because workers control the technology. (In fact, as Roy Morrison and others note, the environmental record of firms such as the Mondragon cooperative system is mixed.) Fourth, since the workers live locally, Schweickart contends they will be less apt to pollute their own communities: While this is probably true, many environmental problems can be displaced to other communities, and worker enterprises operating within a market context would have incentive to do so. Simply put, worker-owned firms operating within a fully competitive market do not inherently "internalize the externalities"—the full costs of social production—although, as noted, after-the-fact regulation of such firms is likely to be significantly more effective in the Schweickart model than under capitalism.

Still, Schweickart's model does contain a mechanism that could substantially strengthen an ecological strategy based on the intrinsic advantages of worker firms: the community banks which disperse capital to firms at the local level. If such banks, at the urging of the local community or because their managers are directly elected by the public, incorporated serious ecological criteria into all "grant-giving," with strict penalties for firms which violated the guidelines, then much of the negative pressures generated by the need for worker firms to cut costs in a competitive market could be alleviated. Clearly, communities with strict criteria would risk at some point damaging their local economies, but the guarantee of new investment funds each year should assure that a community cannot literally regulate itself to death. In general, effective community control over how and to whom capital is disbursed in the first place seems a more promising strategy for attaining serious ecological progress than relying on the still largely untested virtues of worker firms.

Moreover, Schweickart is open to question on three further points regarding ecology: First, what about worker-owned firms in industries that are inherently destructive or unsustainable (such as oil extraction or automobiles)? They would be strongly resistant to shifts to more sustainable industry and would attempt to wield political power in support of their position. Second, while overall economic inequality will likely lessen as returns to capital are more widely distributed, worker-owned systems are still likely to generate wide variance in economic rewards, even among similarly-skilled workers, depending on the exigencies of the market. Such variance is likely to lead to the continuation of some invidious comparisons and a general sense of needing to "keep up with the Joneses." These factors, combined with the fact that one could lose much of what one has if his or her firm goes down (although public jobs of last resort would be guaranteed to all), are likely to generate pressures for getting "more"—both as individuals, and as a society—which could counteract some of the positive ecological features of the Schweickart model. Third, while Schweickart correctly points to the need for urban redesign to reduce long-term transportation and hence energy costs, he is strangely silent in *Against Capitalism* on the issue of local land ownership, even though who owns the land is clearly a key variable in determining whether local-level ecological redesign is politically possible.

Market Socialism Rejected: The Economics of "Participatory Planning"

Michael Albert and Robin Hahnel

The Political Economy of Participatory Economics. Princeton: Princeton University Press, 1991.
Looking Forward: Participatory Economics for the 21st Century. Boston: South End Press, 1991.

Albert and Hahnel completely reject the market socialist approach and instead sketch out a system where the bulk of consumption and all investment and job assignment decisions are made consensually by citizens participating in a democratic process. Each consumer, for instance, would submit their proposed bundle of basic goods to be consumed and work to be performed for a given time period to a neighborhood block; the neighborhood would then come up with its proposed consumption and work plan. After a round of back and forth negotiating between individuals and the neighborhood, the proposals would filter up to the city and regional level, again negotiating back and forth between the higher and lower levels. Finally, the region's proposals would be then fed into a central computer network which would spit out several consumption/production alternatives for the economy amongst which citizens could choose, via voting.

At its best, Albert and Hahnel conceive this system as consisting of an ongoing dialogue of give and take about who is to do and get what. The emphasis on participation extends not only to the consumption /production planning, but also into the workplace: each worker is to have not a job but a "job complex" which balances creative and noncreative tasks. The strong presumption running throughout this proposal is towards as much equality as possible—in consumption, in workplace power, and in determining the overall shape of the economy (through the participatory planning process).

This proposal is difficult to evaluate given its total abstraction from the present day system, yet it is an intellectually coherent effort to show that the market is not the only *theoretical* mechanism for organizing a modern, complex economy. But, as Thomas Weisskopf has pointed out, it is extremely difficult to see how such a society could be achieved without first passing to a halfway house of democratic, market-utilizing socialism of some type that would begin to change the underlying culture in a more cooperative direction. Schweickart's evaluation of the Albert/Hahnel model's feasibility (and this is not the only criticism possible) is succinct, and would win the approval of most observers in this debate:

"Let us start with the very first step: constructing the consumption list. Jane Doe sits at her computer and types in what she would like to consumer for the year. Albert and Hahnel estimate that this will 'take less than thirty hours spread over the course of three weeks. For most people it won't take as long as filling out income tax forms now.' They assume that she has on hand her computer printout of last year's consumption, to facilitate the process. But where does that come from? At some point, people would have to resolve to keep a daily tally, for a full year, of everything purchased. Everyone would have to keep such a list, all 250 million of us. And all these data would have to be collated and typed into the computer. Do we not have here a feasibility problem of the first order?" [35]

In addition to the feasibility question, it is quite clear that concern for individual liberty is not a strong point of Albert and Hahnel's system. While Albert and Hahnel think that the right to privacy will be largely maintained in the process of writing up one's consumption norms for a year, note that individuals wishing to make nontrivial, mid-year (let alone mid-day!) alterations in their consumption patterns would have to work out a deal with other individuals or the larger community agencies to insure that the changes do not cause a mismatch of supply and demand. It is difficult to imagine many in the developed nations embracing that sort of system. Another sore spot is that the Albert and Hahnel system may restrict the capacity of individuals to break out of social norms and "do their own thing" in their own way: In order to get any commodities, you have to do work that is not simply pleasing to one or two benefactors, as with a struggling artist or inventor operating within market society; rather, the entire community must agree that your "work plan" is worthy of support.

Finally, Albert and Hahnel's almost thoroughly negative assessment of markets runs counter to some empirical evidence, such as that marshaled by Yale sociologist Robert Lane (himself no fan of corporate capitalism), which indicates that in certain circumstances markets can play a positive role in human development, such as in fostering a sense of achievement.

Pat Devine

Democracy and Economic Planning. Cambridge, UK: Polity Press, 1988.
"Market Socialism or Participatory Planning?," *Review of Radical Political Economics*, Fall-Winter 1992.

Devine argues that market socialists (particularly Nove, Miller, and Saul Estrin, who has worked closely with Miller) have confused two basic functions of the market: exchange and "market forces." Exchange consists of the sale of inputs and goods, market forces of investment changes, expansion and decline, and entrepreneurship. Devine agrees with Brus and Laski (see below) that "market forces"—the market as a system of allocating investment, as opposed to the simple operation of trade—impels private ownership of the means of production. The solution then is not to abandon social ownership but market processes (termed by Devine the"the anarchy of production") and substitute a participatory planning mechanism. This mechanism is conceived in a similar spirit as the Albert and Hahnel model, but focuses on investment instead of consumption decisions.

It should be noted here that Devine does not take account of the Schweickart market socialist model for democratically allocating investment directly, or the Roemer method of pegging interest rates at different levels for different goods. Instead, he skillfully shows how Nove, Miller, and others fall into contradiction by leaving the bulk of the investment processes to the market's free hand, while hoping somehow to come up with a more desirable overall social result (i.e., no abandoned communities). Devine probably exaggerates the case: The Schweickart model does seem to have some hope for maintaining community stability, and even Roemer's scheme could encourage, say, green technology, while placing huge interest rates on advertising firms.

In Devine's own model, ownership rights are invested in those who are effected by an enterprise's decisions. Thus enterprises are governed day-to-day by boards consisting of workers, consumer representatives, representatives from the local communities in which the firms exist, and the larger planning body. This board sets the prices and insures that production meets consumer demand. There are no profits, as price is set at cost. (This raises questions about what wage levels will be set—wouldn't there be a huge annual battle between worker reps and consumer reps?)

Investment decisions, however, take place in a process of negotiated coordination involving all the interests affected by the proposed change: local communities, workers, suppliers, consumers, environmentalists, and other industry enterprises. The coordinating bodies would take into account both purely economic information and relevant social information, coming to a decision either by consensus, or majority vote when necessary. The big questions are how much weight will be given to each interest by the coordinating boards, and how it would be decided who gets to sit on each board (that is, the fixed bodies considering all the decisions in a given industry). Devine proposes that national level planning priorities be set by a parliamentary body, elected according to proportional representation procedures, after a long process of public dialogue about the public's needs. This national body would also take responsibility for setting the prices of basic inputs, as an indicative guide to the planning process. However, the concrete responsibility for meeting local needs (such as full employment) would lie with local planning bodies, working in cooperation with regional coordinating boards.

Devine writes, "Since decisions are ultimately taken by majority voting, it is clear that I make no assumption that participatory democracy means there will always be agreement. Nevertheless, it is fair to expect that a decision-making process in which all those affected participated would lead to greater understanding of the different interests involved and would generate a dynamic toward compromise and consensus." [36] Devine intends for the model to be "transformatory," that is, to point to a different set of social relations based on cooperation rather than narrow self-interest.

Devine provides relatively discussion of the basis for efficiency within his socialist enterprise or what its internal organization would look like, and leans to a considerable extent on the possibility of a different set of community-oriented motivations for human behavior coming into being; but Devine does count the presence of consumers and other non-worker interests on enterprise boards in a "cross-cutting" fashion as one key source of discipline.

David McNally. *Against the Market: Political Economy, Market Socialism, and the Marxist Critique*. London: Verso, 1992.

McNally rejects market socialism as a theoretical possibility by revisiting Marx's arguments against Proudhon and 19th century versions of "petite bourgeoisie" socialism. McNally's essential point is that the conversion of concrete human labor into an abstract commodity via the market process opens the door to exploitation; hence the market is inconsistent with Marxian socialism. McNally's argument in fact echoes that of N. Scott Arnold: market socialism cannot solve the problem of "exploitation" of labor. However, Arnold is concerned with exploitation arising from distortion of traditional neoclassical incentives, not the Marxian emphasis on capitalist capture of surplus value from labor. Similarly, McNally's perspective mirrors the findings of Brus and Laski: constructing a halfway house that can reconcile markets with socialism is impossible.

In his final chapter, McNally moves the argument from Marx vs. Proudhon to a critique of contemporary versions of market socialism, using Alec Nove as his paradigmatic opponent. What must be rejected is not simply the negative outcomes associated with capitalist markets, but the market process itself which translates human labor into a commodity. Commenting on worker-owned firms, McNally notes:

> The key issue is the compulsion to competitive accumulation which entails the domination of living labour by dead labour—something which can occur even within a worker-managed firm producing for exchange. The struggle for socialism is thus not just, or even principally, about the struggle against a certain group of capitalists, however crucial that may be as point of departure. More important, it is about overturning capital—the system of wage-labour and its basic, dynamic, competitive accumulation.[37]

McNally, much in the spirit of Albert and Hahnel, thus envisions a system of democratic decision making about production and consumption priorities involving all of society. McNally calls for the uniting of "'freely associated producers' in a democratic process in which they regulate and plan the expenditure of human labour and the utilization of means of production in order to satisfy freely expressed needs." [38] Complex computer programs could play an essential role in calculating "planning prices" to help guide such decisionmaking. While McNally does not spell out precisely how his model would work, and says even less about how such a social arrangement would come about, he does, following Marx's enthusiasm for shortening the work week and labor-owned factories in the mid-19th century, admit that current reformist struggles are the place to start. Much of his thinking is consistent with the participatory planning concept developed by Albert and Hahnel. But McNally does allow that market mechanisms "subordinated to socialist planning" could play a role in real socialism.

In the end, McNally's hard rap against market socialism is surely correct to state that "market socialism thus means 'socialism' with wage-labour and exploitation." [39] The conclusion drawn by McNally, that market socialism is therefore "a non-socialism," is a matter of semantics and ideology. McNally has not shown that the market socialist proposals discussed here are implausible: only that they would not meet strong requirements of a thorough-going socialism in which exploitation and class division were wholly abolished.

It remains incumbent upon McNally and like-minded Marxists to show how one could move to a wholly participatory socialism that fulfilled the most stringent requirements of Marx's visions without passing through "reform" stages perhaps not unlike "market socialism." McNally simply does not take up the point raised by Thomas Weisskopf in regard to Albert and Hahnel: that the institutions of "market socialism" could have the plausible effect of achieving a minimal level of egalitarianism that would help strengthen the near-extinct notion of real "equality" by teaching that all deserve a share of the fruits of the economic system. Such an ideological shift would make for a modestly more decent society in the medium-term, and would lay the groundwork for possible, much-later shifts to more radical, nonmarket forms of production and consumption consistent with Marx's loftiest visions. For that reason, even hard-edged Marxists should take "market socialist" thinkers seriously, even if they blanche at affording such proposals the label "socialism."

Michael Barratt Brown. *Models in Political Economy*, Second Edition. New York: Penguin, 1995.

Brown's book has two functions. First, it provides an exceptionally useful introductory description of eleven "models" of the capitalist economy, from neoclassical and monetarist views to Marxist, feminist, and Green critiques, as well as both theoretical and empirical descriptions of four forms of "actually existing socialism" in the 20th century (Soviet, Chinese, Yugoslav, and African). Second, Brown forwards his own version of post-Soviet socialism within the British context, a model which emphasizes small scale and, like Albert and Hahnel, seeks to replace the price mechanism and markets for most forms of economic decision making.

Borrowing from the work of Paul Cockshott and Allin Cottrell, Brown argues that new computer technologies make it possible to replace market pricing of commodities with a system based on the calculation of needed human labor inputs for each product. All forms of labor should be valued equally, and exchange values of goods should be based on how much labor was needed to produce them, as well as how many natural resources were consumed, etc. This way workers who happened to be in high value-added industries would not gain at the expense of other workers (a critical flaw in the Yugoslav model, according to Brown). Brown argues that is quite plausible to use computers to track how much labor and resource inputs are required for each product and to publicize how many resources and how much labour different districts are using.

Brown strongly favors a principle of "subsidiarity," of reducing the scale of government and enterprise management to the smallest workable scale. Large-scale industries could be nationalized, but smaller-scale industries in services, he says, should be owned by a mix of municipal enterprises, cooperatives, and very small private businesses. Each ward of 2,500 people would own its own land and earn rents, as well as provide housing, recreational facilities, and other very small operations. Districts of 50,000 people would provide for public works, small factories, health care, and primary education. Counties of 1,000,000 people would provide police, universities, etc. Regional governments of 6 million would own regional banks and large factories. "Nations" of 110 to 130 million people would be responsible for national infrastructure such as communications and a few large public enterprises. Finally, a "federation of nations," involving perhaps 400 million people would provide defense and certain other large-scale functions. At each level of government, revenues from government-owned enterprises would be a critical source of funds; national and "federation" taxes would also be collected, with disbursements made to the smaller units of government.

Within this system, each unit of government would debate "alternative mixes of possible resource allocations," to be decided upon democratically. Immediate consumption needs would be balanced against an agreed-upon set of environmental standards which had to be adhered to, no matter what plan was adopted. (Unlike Albert and Hahnel, Brown does not discuss individuals submitting their own consumption requests to a planning process; presumably, he envisions that some form of currency—payment for labor—will operate, allowing individuals to make their consumer purchases of available goods. To be decided socially are which goods, and how many, will be available.) Until such time as the larger world economy also adopted a valuation system based on labor input, deals regarding terms of international trade would have to be cut and payments presumably made in real currency. However, in the long term, changing to a labor valuation system as the basis for trade would promote increased equality on a global scale. The low-tech agricultural laborer in Africa whose crop took 40 hours to produce could exchange her product for that of a British high-tech manufacturer, perhaps a TV set, which also took 40 (technology-aided) labor hours to produce. (Brown does not discuss whether obliterating the competitive advantage generated by time-saving technologies might dampen the development of new technologies. Loss of competitive advantage would also likely be a source of political opposition to the labor values system for international trade in the wealthier nations, even in egalitarian regimes, just as the simple self-interest of well-paid professionals would be in establishing such a system in present nonegalitarian countries.)

Brown warns that he is not proposing a totalistic model—some money or currency would still have to be used—and he notes that "[t]he mistake of nearly all model-makers in the past has been to suppose that there was one single cause of all our troubles and therefore one solution for them, instead of a plurality of causes and of ways of prospering." [40] The model Brown lays out where different levels of government operate their own enterprises, down to small local communities, is quite attractive, although it is possible to move in this direction and retain the price system of exchange. By laying out where movement towards a post-capitalist society should start, with local communities owning productive assets directly amidst a rich mix of ownership forms, Brown also helps, perhaps inadvertently, show how a "market socialism"-style model might eventually underpin an experimental shift into participatory planning based on a computer generated list of different alternatives. (Still, the many practical questions about such a system raised by Schweickart and others should not be forgotten.)

Brown is also convincing in suggesting that really generating a society and world in which the economic system generated strong equality as a matter of course—beyond providing each and all minimum incomes, more free time, and a share of community profits, as many market socialist models propose—would eventually require a system of exchange that valued everyone's labor inputs equally. Again, however, such a truly utopian outcome could probably only be the result of long evolutionary experience with more democratic forms of ownership, planning, and politics itself that assumed the price exchange system as the backdrop.

Mixed Economy "Market Socialism"

Alec Nove. *The Economics of Feasible Socialism*. London: George Allen & Unwin, 1983, 1991.

Nove proposes a society with five types of economic organization:

1) Centralized state enterprise, under central control. This sector would include industries which intrinsically require large scale (such as automobile manufacturing), banks and credit institutions, and natural monopolies (i.e. public utilities), as well as the normal functions of government.
2) State-owned enterprises with autonomy from central control and maximal worker participation, working within a competitive market. These enterprises are to compete with each other. Nove does not specify whether there will be hard or soft budget constraints in this sector or what role threat of bankruptcy will play. What this amounts to is a proposal to have the central state take responsibility for profits and losses, as well as provision of credit, in this sector, while hoping that the day-to-day management can be done on a decentralized basis.
3) Workers' cooperatives—medium and small sized businesses owned collectively by its workers, which would receive no special buttress against market competition.

4) Small private enterprise—mom and pop small businesses and retail outlets.

5) Individuals—including the self-employed, consultants, and so forth.

Further, Nove envisions a large role for government planning of major public investments, although the precise goals this planning will achieve are unclear.

As others have noted, Nove presents more of a sketch than an actual blueprint. Competition is supposed to keep his form of market socialism efficient, and Nove cites the Mondragon cooperative system as evidence that the self-managed state sector could be efficient. Nove thinks it could be possible to devise collective material incentives along similar lines within the state enterprise, and believes that equality of wages and meaningful participation in work will be valuable spurs in themselves. Threats from the central state of termination of credit and shutting down the firm would also presumably spur efficiency.

Lane Kensworthy has cast doubt on the possibility of this "independent" state-owned sector really being autonomous from the central state, citing the failure of Hungarian "partial reform" socialism in the 1970s and 80s and the fact that the central state would control all credit in Nove's proposal. In the economy as a whole, Nove judges that the continued existence of "buyer's markets" for consumer goods—in contrast to the Soviet experience, where many commodities were scarce—would be the key to reasonably efficient production of goods that people will actually want.

Overall, the idea that you could flip property arrangements in the modern mixed economy and leave the market structure intact without strongly negative economic results is probably correct. The debate about "feasible" socialism, however, has now gone far beyond Nove.

Samuel Bowles, David Gordon, and Thomas Weisskopf

After the Wasteland. Armonk, NY: M.E.Sharpe, Inc. 1990.
Thomas Weisskopf, "Toward A Socialism of the Future, In the Wake of the Demise of the Socialism of the Past," *Review of Radical Political Economics*, Fall-Winter 1992.

After the Wasteland is oriented towards a radical social democratic economic program, not a full-blown alternative system. The book does impinge on the debate in a number of ways, most notably by effectively compiling the evidence that greater worker participation and ownership boost productivity and efficiency, and that greater worker control over enterprises would be a desirable microeconomic component of an efficient socialist economy.

The basic contention is quoted here at length:

"...[T]here is no substitute for positive work motivation: in contrast to the carrot, the stick is costly to wield and in some jobs is actually counterproductive...Where jobs are routine and easily monitored— as on an assembly line—the stick works. But only a tiny minority of the U.S. labor force are assembly-line workers. Where the quality of the job is subject to subtle variations that are often difficult to detect, and where work is done in groups so that individual inputs are hard to monitor, the carrot is indispensable...

The most certain route to a positive work motivation is virtually self-evident: give the worker a stake in the job. According to this logic, the person who does the work should participate in its design and own the results of his or her labor. Most modern technologies, which require relatively large groups to work together, preclude individual ownership of separate production units. The closest approximation to the ideal of self-ownership and self-direction, therefore, is an economy of firms each no larger than necessary to take advantage of the economies of scale offered by the relevant technology, and each owned and democratically controlled by those who work in them.

The positive incentive to work effectively...is further enhanced by peer pressure from fellow workers...[this] contributes to a reduced need for a structure of surveillance and supervision in the workplace. Additionally, because worker-owned and -managed firms rely heavily on the carrot rather than the stick, unemployment would lose its central role in disciplining labor...

On purely efficiency grounds, the capitalist arrangement is counterproductive, since it gives the least control and the least positive incentive to the workers while it is precisely the quality and intensity of the workers' labor that matters most for enterprise productivity." [41]

Bowles et al do not address the externality problem, or the common argument that an entire economy of labor-managed firms would underutilize labor. But they appear to have a solid point on the micro-level productivity and efficiency issue. It also seems likely that a community-owned firm structure (public enterprise) could capture most of these "positive incentives," even if workers get no separate profits as workers beyond what they get as citizens. If it were efficient to give them a bonus profit stream as workers, the public could democratically install such a system.

Elsewhere, Weisskopf has begun to sketch his version of market socialism, with somewhat less attention to institutional details than other writers have provided. Weisskopf, has, however, provided answers to common objections to market socialist ideas, drawing on insights in the literature as a whole, and has also engaged in an effective polemic against Albert and Hahnel's more radical vision. Weisskopf himself favors some form of joint worker/citizen claim on profits—a two-tiered approach—within a market system with a strong welfare state and strong macro-level economic planning.

Curtis Moore. *Constitution for a Democratic Economy—The econ. democracy news group.*

Drawing from the American left communitarian literature on economics, Moore has sketched in some detail a "constitution" for a democratic economy. Moore leans particularly heavily on the work of Samuel Bowles, David Gordon, and Thomas Weisskopf, Martin Carnoy and Derek Shearer, Gar Alperovitz and Jeff Faux, and J.W. Smith's *The World's Wasted Wealth*, as well as many other authors, in formulating his own systematic blueprint. Further, Moore's constitution is not a fixed publication but instead appears as an internet newsgroup (econ.democracy) hosted by the Institute for Global Communications, a progressive internet service provider. His constitution is updated and refined on a regular basis, and persons visiting the conference are free to comment on any aspect of Moore's presentation.

Moore's basic conception is of a full employment economy that provides a guaranteed minimum income to all citizens, provided citizens work the equivalent of two-thirds of a year on a full time basis. At the same time, Moore stresses minimizing the cost of basic necessities (housing, energy, etc.) through public subsidies, "demonetization" (i.e. seeking to provide necessities outside the paid economy), and controls on prices in the necessities sector such that the necessities cost no more than one-fourth of the minimal annual income. (Moore likens the demonetization concept to a military base economy, where necessities are provided to soldiers free of charge, as part of the salary. In other words, Moore wants to incorporate as many necessities as possible into the society's publicly provided goods.)

To make the full employment process work, Moore would establish in each county, state, and the nation at large "Citizen Assemblies," which would be charged with making an inventory of public needs in each locality. This information would be used by a public planning agency at the national level to generate a list of public spending priorities. The goal would be for the needed work to always outpace the number of people required to do it, so that if unemployment emerges, one could simply take a project "off the shelf" to effect a return to full employment.

Moore proposes an essentially mixed economy, calling for widespread public ownership, but not public monopolies in any industry. Rather, the public, including not only government-owned firms but worker coops, nonprofits, etc., should hold a meaningful stake in each key sector of the economy and act alongside private firms. Their central purpose would be to serve as a brake against recessions. The "public" sector would be mandated to produce a fixed amount of product per year, regardless of what else happened in the economy, thereby serving as a check against industrywide downturns. If private firms in a sector cut back employment and production, the public firms would be instructed to increase their expenditures. Essentially, this is a Keynesian concept of countercyclical spending, except that the public expenditure would take place in goods-producing industries, not just government projects.

Apart from these features, Moore's constitution covers a comprehensive range of economic topics, including health care provision, transportation, democratizing the Federal Reserve Board and making credit for small enterprises available to all citizens on a periodic basis, chartering corporations, trade policy, alternative economic indicators, wage and price controls, and so forth. Moore admits at the outset that creating an actual "constitution" for a different economy ought to be a collective process, the result of a constitutional convention, and cannot be the work of any single author. Still, Moore finds that the constitution concept is a good way to specify and clarify a set of wide-ranging ideas and eventually make them more accessible to the public.

Moore has not in his conference delved deeply into theories of social change; nor does Moore take up the problem that a mixed economy regime in which private corporations still have a major role, even if restraints are implemented, will likely lead to considerable political instability and leave the door open to rolling back the progressive reforms Moore envisions.

Indeed, it is difficult to imagine how so wide-ranging a document as Moore has sketched would ever be adopted in a society in which profit-seeking corporations enjoyed substantial political and economic power. It might seem that drawing up effective constitutions for a different economy is something that must happen "after the revolution," that is, after first constraining, then breaking up, and finally spinning off large-scale corporate entities to different institutional forms. But specifying exactly what legal and constitutional changes would be needed to implement a full-fledged democratic economy could result in a useful tool for public discussion—and demonstrate that the ideas of those who support alternatives to present-day capitalism can be "operationalized," that is, made to work as a coherent whole in the real world.

Revisionist and Pessimistic Market Socialism

Wlodzimierz Brus and Kazimierz Laski. *From Marx to the Market: Socialism in Search of an Economic System.* Oxford: Clarendon Press, 1989.

This is the book that scares other market socialist theorists. After an extremely cogent and useful account of the pluses and minuses of Soviet economic development and of the Hungarian and Yugoslavian reform models, Brus and Laski paint a picture of a fully reformed market socialist system, with complete enterprise autonomy from the state, a capital market, and a managerial "market" providing the same stimulus to efficiency (top-down) as under capitalism. The problem is entrepreneurship—getting socialist managers to deal with "market processes" as efficiently as do capitalists. (Here again, market processes mainly refers to investment decisions.) They conclude that if people aren't risking their own money, it is difficult to obtain the benefits of entrepreneurship. This leads to the following question: "What actually are the advantages of getting state enterprises to imitate the behavior of private ones through enormous and by no means assuredly successful efforts, or of devising bewilderingly complex schemes to make individuals act as entrepreneurs without becoming owners?" [42]

Their response is to keep the answer "open-ended"; perhaps there are good reasons to keep a strong state role in enterprise management, but they are not yet convinced of them. In the meantime, their 1989 hope was that

74

Eastern Europe could evolve into some form of mixed economy in which market socialist ideas would be tried on a pragmatic basis. Brus and Laski did not foresee, experiments with "coupon socialism" and worker-owned firms aside, the rapidity with which former East Bloc nations would embrace capitalism in the 1990s.

Global Solutions

Arjun Makhijani. *From Global Capitalism to Economic Justice.* New York: Apex Press, 1992.

Makhijani's "inquiry into the elimination of systemic poverty, violence, and environmental destruction in the world economy" echoes many of the themes noted in the first two chapters of this bibliography. His book calls for "democratic control" over large corporations, argues that the case for capitalism's success has been badly overstated, shows that socialist government can be workable by citing the well-known Kerala state government in India, and calls for building self-reliant communities through democratic economic planning at a local scale.

Makhijani's unique contribution, however, is a highly convincing proposal to reform the international currency system so that currency values reflect the actual productivity of a nation's workers. The present floating exchange rate system, in which "exchange rates are determined primarily by the prices and quantities of commodities that are imported," results in a gross discrepancy between, for instance, what a peso can buy in real goods in Mexico, and what it can buy in real goods across the border in San Diego. International organizations and economists have long been aware of this discrepancy, and have responded by creating "purchasing power parity" indexes to measure the real buying power of national currencies. For instance, the per capita GNP of Mexico, converted to U.S. dollars based on prevailing exchange rates, was $3,837 in 1994. But the actual amount of per capita purchasing power in Mexico was equivalent to $7,239. Simply put, bread and rice and tortillas are cheaper in Mexico than in the United States. Hence, the "per capita GNP" figure grossly undervalues the real productivity of the Mexican economy.

This undervaluation, as Makhijani points out, has two serious detrimental effects. First, it means Mexico has to pay nearly twice as much for goods from the United States as it would in a "barter" system, or other system based on actual productivity of the economy. Second, it creates an artificial incentive for American capital to move to Mexico to take advantage of cheap labor, cheapness nearly doubled by the weakness of the peso relative to the Mexican economy's productivity. Mexico is the most striking example of a phenomenon common to the entire global "south": Currency values do not reflect comparative productivities, and the poorer nations get the short end of the stick.

Makhijani thus proposes to root currency values in actual labor productivity, not in the flows of supply and demand on the highly speculative currency market, or, as a de facto consequence of American monetary policy (the dollar being the guiding standard for international trade). Exchange rates—pesos to dollars—are to be determined based on the "relative prices of basic consumer goods in each country." A new International Currency Unit, with a fixed purchasing power wherever used, would replace the dollar as the core currency unit. Each country then would be required to "back" its currency by setting aside a reserve of core commodity stocks. Above-average labor productivity increases would make currency values rise. Makhijani provides a brief technical description of how the "basket of consumer goods" acting as the basis for currency values could be constructed to avoid comparing, say, South American beans and rice with OECD chicken and cheese.

Makhijani argues that this system would increase the real purchasing power on the global market—the terms of trade—for the world's poor countries; drastically increase the wages of workers in the south; permit countries to pursue development policies without fear of being knocked down by the currency markets; and lead to a much more stable system of international trade, benefitting both rich and poor countries. Makhijani envisions a coalition of third world and some OECD countries endorsing this type of plan and calling for a new Bretton Woods conference to reorient the world monetary system; he admits that the likely opposition of the American government would be a giant obstacle to attaining a reconfigured global trading system.

Thomas Pogge. "Radical International Inequalities and the Global Resource Tax," in David Crocker and Toby Linden, eds., *Ethics of Consumption: The Good Life, Justice, and Global Stewardship.* Lanham, MD: Rowman and Littlefield, 1997.

Columbia University philosopher Thomas Pogge advocates an even more direct measure for redistributing resources among rich and poor nations: Collecting a fixed tax on primarily nonrenewable, but also renewable, natural resources, to be paid into a trust fund used to finance basic development programs in poorer nations. Those who extract the resources would be charged the tax; for instance, Kuwait would pay a tax an oil extracted. Pogge expects the resource extractors would raise the prices to recoup the value of the tax (thus providing a consumer disincentive to consume scarce resources). Pogge estimates that a fully implemented Global Resource Tax (GRT) pegged at 1% of world GNP would generate $270 billion a year (as of 1994). This money would be distributed by a central global body to poor nations. In countries where governments are too corrupt, international aid agencies would be given the money to carry out concrete development projects, aimed at improving the well-being of the poor.

Pogge acknowledges that many practical problems would arise from trying to implement a Global Resource Tax, notably effective enforcement measures. As for convincing the richer nations to implement this scheme, Pogge simply forwards a strategy of persuading citizens of rich countries that their own interests would be well-served by uplifting the living conditions of the poor. Further, it might even be possible to strike a grand bargain between north and south in which the north agrees to a GRT in exchange for the cooperation of poorer nations in containing the proliferation of dangerous technologies, namely weapons of mass destruction.

Pogge's proposal is attractive on paper, but unfortunately citizens in the United States in particular are not well-disposed towards the concept of substantive international sharing, and this is likely to be the case so long as many Americans themselves feel economically insecure. Implementing a scheme like Pogge's would probably require first providing a basic modicum of security, as well as establishing a precedent of sharing wealth, within the richer countries—especially the United States. Nevertheless, Pogge's approach is a logical extension of many of the suggested mechanisms to reconfigure the distribution of wealth within advanced capitalist regimes noted elsewhere in this volume.

Market Socialism Evaluated

N. Scott Arnold. *The Philosophy and Economics of Market Socialism.* New York: Oxford University Press, 1994.

Arnold's critique of various market socialist proposals is sympathetic yet harsh. Focusing (rather narrowly) on the problem of "exploitation" within market socialist economies, exploitation being defined in the technical sense of persons not being rewarded according to the value of their contributions. Arnold identifies six ends which an economy conforming to the "socialist conception of the good society" should meet:

1) The achievement of a reasonable standard of living
2) The end of alienation in the workplace
3) The collective control of the rate and direction of economic growth and development
4) The prevention or correction of the social irrationalities that would otherwise arise from the operation of the market (including, for instance, 'commodity fetishism')
5) The elimination of exploitation
6) The achievement of (relative) equality of material condition.[43]

If an economy cannot meet these tests, according to Arnold, it cannot be said to conform to the socialist conception of the good society. Arnold sets his sights particularly tightly on the difficult stipulation of the "elimination of exploitation." Advocates of labor-managed market socialism believe that capitalist exploitation of labor will be essentially ended in a labor-managed regime, but even if this were so, Arnold states, other forms of exploitation would arise. For instance, in a system of labor-owned firms, more egalitarian pay scales would mean that higher skilled employees would tend to be paid less than the value of their work and thus "exploited" by their lower-skilled colleagues. Arnold provides the example of a skilled diamond cutter and a janitor getting nearly equal wages at a labor-managed diamond coop.

To be paid at one's value, however, can have two very distinct meanings: It might mean 1) that one's pay is equivalent to the marginal contribution one makes to the finished product—the wages=MC equilibrium of neoclassical economics; or 2) that one is paid at a rate equivalent to the pay one's skills could demand on the open market. The essence of the standard Marxist critique of capitalism is that because labor is usually not scarce, value #2 tends to be less than #1, meaning that capitalists can hire workers to work for less than the contribution of their value to the finished product. On the other hand, current pay of CEOs in the United States is only rarely defended on the grounds that the managers actually contribute as much as they earn, but on grounds that the market scarcity of managerial talent makes firms willing to pay CEOs large premiums.

Arnold, however, rejects the Marxian account of the exploitation of labor, and instead offers a neoclassical definition of fair exchange: Workers are only being exploited if they are not paid according to their market value at any given moment, and they have no opportunities to take another job which would pay their market value. If accepted, this conception almost tautologically rules out the possibility of a generalized exploitation of labor, but Arnold's position fails to convince. To provide a simple counter-example, workers in Mexico in an auto factory may be just as productive, contribute just as much to the total value of an automobile, as workers in Detroit, yet be paid only one-fifth as much as their American counterparts. According to Arnold, no exploitation would be present in this case, even though the wages paid to the Mexican workers almost certainly would be less than the contribution to the final product the workers made.

Aside from the example of the highly skilled worker being underpaid, Arnold also shows ways in which managers and owners of capital might be "exploited" by labor-managed firms under market socialism, and in turn how state organizations might exploit the cooperatives. Arnold frequently notes that these problems do not exist under capitalism. Arnold states that the existence of this sort of exploitation in the system will lead some to try to "rip it off," undermining the legitimacy and stability of the system. As in state socialism, a class of opportunists would emerge. But those convinced that capitalism depends on a generalized exploitation of labor are not likely to be swayed in their assessment of market socialism by Arnold's identification of these seemingly minor instances of "exploitation."

In any case, Arnold's entire discussion of exploitation hinges on the traditional economic notion that individuals (capitalists or labor) create wealth and deserve to get what they create. The "community inheritance" notion developed by Gar Alperovitz (and suggested by many others) stresses the extent to which most current wealth is a collective product inherited from the past by those now alive, who did *nothing* to earn it. What sense does it make to speak of the right of the skilled diamond cutter to keep the value of his or her contribution if the skill of cutting diamonds, and the long educational and technical buildup of this skill, is itself a free gift from the past? (Not to mention the rock itself!) He or she cuts the stone, but cannot be said to have created the skill itself; the cutter has been trained by the community to use the inherited skill, hence the community should take an appropriate share of the fruits of the cutting.

For all this, Arnold's book is still a thoughtful, important analysis, even if his rigidly neoclassical outlook on market exchange understandably leaves many of his conversation partners (such as Schweickart) cold. Arnold does well in analyzing the likely tensions that would emerge in trying to graft egalitarian institutions onto a populace radically unequal in skills and education. Beyond the "exploitation" problem, Arnold argues that market socialist proposals will have difficulty eradicating inequality, collectively controlling the direction of economic development, or eliminating market irrationalities. Arnold forcefully concludes that any workable variation of market socialism probably will violate the "socialist conception of the good society" due to exploitation, but he allows that if such a conception is abandoned, market socialist proposals could be defensible on other philosophic grounds. "That may be a project with some success," Arnold notes, "but it would require one to give up on socialism, both as an economic system and as a vision of the good society." [44]

Christopher Pierson. *Socialism After Communism: The New Market Socialism*. Oxford: Oxford University Press, 1995.

After an obligatory 75 page requiem and meditation upon state socialism and the current "crisis of socialism," Pierson succinctly analyzes the key elements of the various market socialist proposals that have been put on the table (including especially Miller, Schweickart, Nove, Roemer, Yunker and Saul Estrin). Pierson summarizes the key contentions of market socialist writers as follows:

- There is no alternative to the market as the principal mode of organization for a modern economy.
- Markets (including labor markets and differential wages) promote efficiency, in general.
- The market promotes liberty and makes autonomy—and genuine self-management—possible; given that some redistribution is needed to maximize positive freedom for all.

- The market may be necessary for democracy, but capitalism is not. Capitalism gives disproportionate political power to the representatives of capital, and does not permit broad "democratic" control of the priorities and purpose of the economy (as many of these thinkers hope will be possible under market socialism. See discussion of Roemer and "indicative planning" above). Finally, under capitalism, democracy is not extended to perhaps the most important sphere of social production—the workplace.
- Social justice requires a market of some type—or else there is no way to ensure people are appropriately compensated for their contribution (not "exploited").

The proposed structure of market socialism, Pierson notes, generally consists of some form of socially-owned, but not state-administered, enterprises operating within a market and returning income to worker-owners, the state, or some combination thereof. Small-scale entrepreneurial capitalists are tolerated and even encouraged, but not permitted to evolve into modern-type corporations. Capital is dispensed not via a capital market but by some form of public banking system. Inequality is not to be eradicated but moderated, either by the more equal wage scale one would expect under worker self-management (in *some* of the models), or by disbursement of social dividends from the public profits of socially owned enterprises. The state continues to provide the familiar welfarist functions and to give partial, but not comprehensive, guidance to the economy.

Pierson goes on to elaborate a number of useful critiques of market socialism from both left and right. First, elements of the left and right agree that markets are fundamentally incompatible with socialism. From the left, these claims fall into seven categories, Pierson notes:

- Markets generate (massive) inequality.
- Markets are inequitable—unfair in terms of rewarding merit and effort, as well as in meeting needs
- Under markets, management exploits workers
- Markets generate inefficiency and waste
- The market undermines democracy
- The market denies the capacity to exercise positive freedom (to many but not all)
- The market promotes anti-social individualism.

For critiques two through six, Pierson notes, market socialists would insist that once capitalist power has been removed from the market (and perhaps some planning added), the critiques would no longer hold up. As to the first and last points, most theorists admit that market socialism cannot solve the problems but might at least mitigate the worst tendencies.

Turning to the right, Pierson considers the critique of Hayek and others of socialism and the conservative insistence that "social ownership" is just a cloak for state-owned socialism. On the whole Pierson does not find these critiques very compelling, not because of any logical flaw, but because the picture Hayek et al paint of how markets actually work is highly idealized. Pierson believes that market socialism can meet the standard objections of left and right, and even be economically feasible, if it can also be shown to be politically feasible.

Pierson's final judgment is that market socialism is not a politically feasible strategy, at least within developed countries. In part this judgment comes from tactical considerations about the capacity of market socialism as a program to attract an electoral majority; he cites in particular the lack of engagement with feminist and ecological concerns in most market socialist writings. More damning in Pierson's view, however, is the implausibility of state civil servants ever transforming themselves into the administrators of a market socialist economy; this transformation would be at least as politically difficult as attempting to nationalize corporations outright. Even the related strategy of pension-fund socialism, as attempted under the Meidner plan in Sweden to gradually transfer ownership assets to workers, was "when pursued as a strategy within the most trenchantly social democratic polity ever devised...repeatedly watered-down and then effectively abandoned." [45]

Lurking behind these judgments, of course, is an acute awareness that perhaps *any* serious Left program is impossible, for one reason or another, in the current and foreseeable political climate. Pierson admits to having no answer of his own, other than a conviction that "socialism" as a broad principle should not be ditched and that future programs should address the themes of more democracy (especially in the workplace), new forms of social ownership, and ecological consciousness. In fact, Pierson is perhaps too much a prisoner of the current signs of the times, as if they will never change, in his cold assessment of the feasibility of market socialism, but his warning of the difficulties is not to be taken lightly.

Additional References

Stanley Aronowitz and William DeFazio. *The Jobless Future*. Minneapolis: University of Minnesota Press, 1994. Aronowitz and DeFazio analyze the rise of job insecurity within a neo-Marxist framework. They urge the reduction of the work week, and more than this, the need to develop a new ethic whereby one's working life plays a less definitive role in constituting identity.

Jeremy Rifkin. *The End of Work*. New York: Tarcher/Putnam, 1995. Rifkin argues to a popular audience that the current downsizing trend is a sign of a much larger historical shift towards an era of inadequate job opportunities. He calls for shortening of the work week, job-sharing, and the development of paid work opportunities in the nonprofit sector.

Robert Lane. *The Market Experience*, 1991. A major event in political science and sociology, this book encapsulates in encyclopedic fashion the results of some four decades of empirical studies on the relationship between market processes and well-being. Lane draws on hundreds of such studies in developing his own argument about how markets do some things well (such as provide a sense of achievement) and many other things very poorly.

Joseph Blasi and Douglas Kruse. *The New Owners: The Mass Emergence of Employee Ownership in Public Companies and What It Means to American Business*. New York: HarperCollins, 1991. Strong empirical data on the trend towards employee stock ownership within corporate America.

Fred Block. *Postindustrial Possibilities*. Berkeley: University of California, 1990. Excellent critique of basic categories of economic analysis. Urges more public goods, reduction of working hours.

Fred Block. *The Vampire State*. New York: The New Press, 1996.

Saul Estrin. *Self-management: Economic Theory and Yugoslav Practice*. Cambridge: Cambridge University Press, 1983.

Edward Greenberg. *Workplace Democracy: The Political Effects of Participation*. Ithaca: Cornell University Press, 1986. Important empirical study of worker ownership's limited capacity to shape broader political and moral values within the context of capitalist society.

Paul Cockshott and Allin Cottrell. *Towards A New Socialism*. Spokesman, 1993.

Roy Morrison. *We Build the Road As We Travel*. Philadelphia: New Society Publishers, 1991.

William Foot Whyte and Kathleen King Whyte. *Making Mondragon: The Growth and Dynamics of the Worker Cooperative Complex*. Ithaca: Cornell University Press, 1988. The Whyte and Morrison books provide celebratory but not uncritical accounts of this complex of worker-owned firms in the Basque region.

Robert Dahl. *A Preface to Economic Democracy*. Cambridge: Polity Press, 1985. Dahl endorses worker-owned firms as a model for the economy, and argues that if one cannot accept democracy in the workplace and the economy, it is unclear why one should accept arguments for democracy in government either.

Jonathan Boswell. *Community and the Economy: The Theory of Public Cooperation*. New York: Routledge, 1990. Boswell advocates a corporatist approach to economic decisionmaking in which government brings all the major players (business, labor, etc.) to the table to forge a social consensus. He specifies the conditions under which this is workable, including relatively small scale—thus the United States is simply too big to make a "cooperative" approach workable, Boswell judges.

Brunko Horvat. *The Political Economy of Socialism*. Armonk, NY: M.E. Sharpe, 1982.

Oskar Lange. "On the Economic Theory of Socialism" (1938). Reprinted in B.Lippincott, ed, *On the Economic Theory of Socialism*. Minneapolis: University of Minnesota Press, 1958.

Donald Lavoie. *Rivalry and Central Planning: The Socialist Calculation Debate Reconsidered*. Cambridge: Cambridge University Press, 1985. Detailed discussion of the Von Hayek-Lange debate of the 1930s, from a libertarian perspective.

Donald Lavoie. *National Economic Planning: What is Left?* Washington: The Cato Institute, 1985. This partisan polemic against advocates of economic planning and market socialism shows how a conservative evaluates proposals for "economic democracy" forwarded by the likes of Carnoy & Shearer, Alperovitz & Faux, etc.

J. Carens. *Equality, Moral Incentives and the Market: An Essay in Utopian Politico-Economic Theory*. Chicago: University of Chicago Press, 1981.

David Ellerman. *The Democratic Worker-owned Firm*. London: Unwin and Hyman, 1990. Especially useful in its attention to the precise institutional rules necessary to prevent worker firms from lapsing into capitalist firms by workers selling out their shares.

Jon Elster and Karl Moene. Eds. *Alternatives to Capitalism.* Cambridge:Cambridge University Press, 1989.

Julian LeGrand and Saul Estrin, eds. *Market Socialism.* Oxford: Clarendon Press, 1989.

Joseph Stiglitz. *Whither Socialism,* 1994. Cambridge: The MIT Press, 1994. Balanced, incisive account of the collapse of socialism, privatization, and the feasibility of market socialist institutions from a cautiously liberal economist. Notable for its defense of public enterprise and positive appraisal of aspects of the Chinese economic system.

Severyn T. Bruyn. *A Future for the American Economy: The Social Market.* Stanford: Stanford University Press, 1991. Urges the development of self-regulating enterprises that will take social and ethical considerations into account in decision-making, by such means as trade associations that coordinate cooperation among firms, worker ownership, and employee participation. Valuable for its emphasis on the social structure of productive organizations as crucial to determining outcomes within a market system.

Ota Sik. *For a Humane Economic Democracy.* New York: Praeger Special Studies, 1985.

Robin Archer. *Economic Democracy: the Politics of Feasible Socialism.* New York: Oxford University Press, 1995.

Martin Carnoy and Derek Shearer. *Economic Democracy.* White Plains, N.Y.: M. E. Sharpe, 1980. Influential but dated statement of how a left social democratic program in the United States might look at both the local and national levels.

Gar Alperovitz and Jeff Faux. *Rebuilding America: A Blueprint for the New Economy.* New York: Pantheon, 1984. The authors emphasize the desirability of economic planning for full employment in each and every community, the development of community-based firms, and how to harmonize full employment policies with the need to restrain inflation.

Adam Przeworski. *Capitalism and Social Democracy.* Cambridge: Cambridge University Press, 1985. Analysis of the crisis of "electoral socialism" in the contemporary West.

Frank Roosevelt and David Belkin, eds. *Why Market Socialism? Voices from Dissent.* Armonk, NY: M.E. Sharpe, 1994. Collected essays from *Dissent* magazine on the subject.

Roberto Mangabeira Unger. *False Necessity*. New York: Cambridge University Press, 1987. Unger develops the idea of a rotating capital fund, in which publicly held capital is auctioned off to users for a fee. Unger's proposal is similar, although more nuanced, to that of Tibor Liska.

Thomas Michael Power. *The Economic Pursuit of Quality*. Armonk, NY: M.E. Sharpe, Inc. 1988. Power's work is oriented towards the development of qualitative, not growth-oriented, goals for local-level economic development as a corrective to market processes. Includes insightful analysis of the role of economic insecurity in the movement towards more consumption at both individual and community level. Strongly compatible with the emphasis on community-rooted local economic development suggested by Alperovitz, others. Updated edition published in 1996 by M.E. Sharpe under the title *Environmental Protection and Economic Well-Being: The Economic Pursuit of Quality*.

Doug Henwood. *Wall Street*. New York: Verso, 1997. Henwood offers a detailed analysis of the world of finance from an anti-capitalist perspective. Though loathe to offer a detailed blueprint, Henwood favors a form of market socialism based on Japanese and German models of banking and corporate ownership.

David Gordon. *Fat and Mean*. New York: The Free Press, 1996. Trenchant analysis pointing to corporate power and union decline, not skills or technology, as the driving motor behind increasing inequality; Gordon presents a five-point proposal for the American economy to take the "high road" of economic development.

Keith Cowling and Roger Sugden. *Beyond Capitalism: Towards a New World Economics Order*. New York: St. Martin's Press, 1994.

Roger Burbach, Orlando Nunez, and Boris Kagarlitsky. *Globalization and Its Discontents: The Rise of Postmodern Socialisms*. London: Pluto Press, 1997.

Michael Perelman. *The Pathology of the U.S. Economy: The Costs of a Low Wage System*. New York: St. Martin's Press, 1993.

Sharryn Kasmir. *The Myth of Mondragon*. Albany: State Unversity of New York Press, 1996.

Chapter Three

Sustainability and the System Problem

Overview

The past three decades have been witness to an explosion in public concern regarding the environment and a concomitant growth of a vast literature regarding environmental affairs. But the fraction of that literature addressing what an alternative *institutional*—not policy—structure conducive to ecologically sustainability might look like is still disproportionately small. The work of the most prominent green thinktanks—the World Resources Institute, the Worldwatch Institute, and various advocacy groups—tends to focus on issues, problems, and policy solutions, with relatively little attention given to the underlying "architectural" issues, much less what an architectural "solution" might look like. Similarly, most thinkers in the deep ecology movement and other radical strands of green thought tend to train their sights on broad-scaled cultural and civilizational criticism instead of analyzing specific power relationships and social structures. Further, green thinkers who do explicitly address issues of power, such as Barry Commoner, have not taken up the question of alternative institutional architecture in a sustained fashion.

This is not to say that the question has been left alone—but rather that it remains relatively underdeveloped. The existing literature can perhaps be neatly divided into two eras: before and after the 1989 publication of Herman Daly and John Cobb's *For the Common Good*. The mid-1970s to mid-1980s saw the publication of a number of attempts to sketch the architecture of a green society, notably those of William Ophuls, German green Rudolf Bahro, French labor intellectual Andre Gorz, and Lester Milbrath. Although insightful, none of these works match the thoroughness and sophistication of Daly and Cobb's *For the Common Good*. That book contains not only an exposition of the notion of a "steady-state" economy but also includes an impressive listing of numerous concrete strategies for achieving such an economy, focusing on the concept of community. Community land ownership, increased local self-reliance and de-linking from global markets, and a rollback of corporate forms in favor of community-based entrepreneurial activity, and more traditional green strategies (such as population stabilization) stand out among Daly and Cobb's proposals. Daly and Cobb's work has stimulated an increased attention to issues of architectural design in recent years (especially among ecological economists and the International Society of Ecological Economists itself).

The literature since Daly and Cobb has expanded their fundamental thrust in two different directions. First, the notion of delinking from the global economy to build local self-reliance is now a commonplace idea among ecological thinkers and activists.* Second, a handful of writers, in particularly Douglas Booth and Gar Alperovitz, have gone beyond Daly and Cobb, forcefully pointing out the contradiction between capitalist institutions and the positive elements of the Daly and Cobb vision. These writers urge that an alternative structure is a fundamental precursor to achieving Daly and Cobb's hoped-for reforms. Other writers, such as Juliet Schor, while still stopping short of direct rejection of capitalist institutions, have also sketched fuller-scale visions of ecologically sustainable economies with obvious debts to Daly and Cobb; in Schor's case the emphasis is on shortened work weeks in advanced capitalist societies. The arguments of these thinkers are detailed below in the annotations.

Most recently, Australian writer and activist Ted Trainer in 1995 offered what is perhaps the most comprehensive guidebook yet of practical strategies and "system thought" aimed at ecological sustainability in his book *The Conserver Society*. Trainer starts with the assumption that present Western economies grossly overconsume and should be built down to more appropriately-scaled, less waste-generating economies. Trainer does not duck the obvious contradiction between this premise and capitalist institutions. Drawing heavily on the emergent literature regarding "permaculture," Trainer proposes a variety of strategies in each sector (agriculture, energy, etc.) to achieve a "conserver society," stressing such institutions as community gardens, community ownership-in-general, and radically reduced workweeks. While the Trainer vision can be criticized as extreme and unbalanced by values other than ecology (such as "liberty"), it is one of the

---

* See Jerry Mander and Edward Goldsmith, eds., *The Case Against the Global Economy and For a Turn Toward the Local* (San Francisco: Sierra Club Books, 1996), for statements of this general point of view from over two dozen analysts and activists.

best examples to date of a radically pessimistic environmental world-view taken to its logical conclusion in terms of the comprehensive impact an awareness of gross ecological imbalance should have on our institutions.

This bibliography also includes discussion of Murray Bookchin, the influential American philosopher of "eco-anarchism," that is, ecological reconstruction based on small communities; British writer David Pepper, who has sought to bridge the gap between Marxist and eco-anarchist approaches in developing his own concept of "eco-socialism"; and Christian ethicist Larry Rasmussen, who has drawn the connections between a holistic systemic analysis of current environmental problems and the resources offered by religious traditions for addressing those problems via the slow work of re-constituting communities on different basic assumptions.

A brief definition of the "steady-state economy," frequently mentioned below, may be in order here: In the strictest sense, a steady-state economy is one that does not expand its use of natural resources (excepting solar energy use that does not also consume land), or its pool of physical capital (such as manufacturing plants, roads, bridges, and so forth). Note carefully, this does not mean that the economy may not grow in the GDP sense, or that technology does not continue to progress. As physical capital is replaced with newer technology it may become more productive; industries (such as the information sector) which do not require expanded resource use to grow may grow; more generally, improved technology may allow us to produce more with less input of resources (just as it has allowed us to produce more with less input of human labor in the past two centuries). In the steady-state such "growth" would be acceptable only on condition of no net increase in resource use. Thus many current industries would likely have to be actively shrunk; and the overall rate of growth would surely be (at least initially) much lower than the current rate. (Indeed, a steady-state economy would have little use for the economic growth rate as a relevant indicator.)

William Ophuls. *Ecology and the Politics of Scarcity Revisited*. New York: W.H. Freeman and Company, 1992. (Updated from 1977 first edition).

Ophuls was one of the first writers to explicitly argue that achieving ecological balance requires a fundamental systemic change, although he does not offer a specific solution institutionally. Instead, he argues first and foremost for the need for a "fundamental transformation of world view" and the development of a different "paradigm." Ophuls' statement of this view is eloquent:

> Current political values and institutions are the products of the age of abnormal abundance now drawing to a close, so any solutions predicated on scarcity would necessarily conflict with them. Of course, to work 'within the system' to prevent further ecological degradation and promote incremental change towards the steady state is an essential task... But to accept current political reality as not itself subject to radical change is to give away the game at the outset and render the situation hopeless by definition... To put it another way, normal politics is indeed 'the art of the possible'; it consists of working as best one can for valued objectives 'within the system'—that is, inside the current political paradigm. However, politicking (to give it its true name) is only one part of politics and the lesser part at that. In its truest sense, politics is the art of new possibilities for human progress. Because the current system is ecologically defective, we must direct our concrete political activities primarily towards producing a change of consciousness that can lead to a new political paradigm. Until people at large begin to see a new kind of reality based on ecological understanding, environmental politicking within the system can be only a rear-guard holding action designed to slow the pace of ecological retreat.[46]

Ophuls stresses that such a transition would take decades, and that the final solution "will be a mosaic of many elements, some designed by dint of human effort, others fashioned by the accidents of history." A concrete blueprint thus can only be formed as part of the process of social learning and in reaction to the emerging dimensions of the ecological crisis. For all this restraint as to programmatic specifics, Ophuls is quite clear on the need for a steady-state economy, and he goes on to note the probable "sociopolitical characteristics of any steady-state society," including:

1) "Communalism," where "the traditional primacy of the community over the individual that has characterized virtually every other

period of history will be restored...the degree of individual subordination (for example, of property rights) that will eventually be required would probably seem quite insupportable to many living today." [47]

2) "Authority," namely, increased state authority over the use of property to enforce ecological norms. Ophuls stresses that no threat to personal and civil liberties is required.

3) "Government." Ophuls writes that "certain restriction on human activities must be competently determined, normatively justified, and then imposed on a populace that would do something quite different if it was left to its own immediate desires and devices... Future political theorists will therefore have to overcome the exceedingly difficult problem of legislating the temperance and virtue needed for the ecological survival of a steady-state society without at the same time exalting the few over the many and subjecting individuals to the unwarranted exercise of administrative power or to excessive conformity to some dogma." [48]

4) "Politics." "[W]e must move from non-politics toward politics. Laissez faire is a device for making political decisions about the distribution of wealth and other desired goods automatically and rather non-politically, instead of in face to face political confrontation....At least at the outset those who live in the steady state will therefore have to be genuinely political animals in Aristotle's sense, self-consciously involved in designing and planning their community life." [49]

5) "Stewardship." "[W]e shall move away from the values of growth, profligacy, and exploitation typical of 'economic man' toward sufficiency, frugality, and stewardship." [50]

6) "Modesty," since, "[O]nce the limitations nature imposes on people have become clearer, Faustian striving after power and 'progress' should give way to modesty of both ends and means...there is no intrinsic reason why a steady-state society, despite its material frugality, should suffer from cultural stagnation, nor is there any reason why personal and cultural life should not be at least as rewarding as it is in today's industrial civilization. But the rewards must necessarily be rather different, for the culture of the steady state will certainly be far more frugal and modest than our own." [51]

7) "Diversity." Ophuls expresses the view that decentralization and local autonomy are more consistent with his core values than centralized governance.

8) "Holism." Ophuls states that systemic thinking must replace narrow, single-dimension thought. Thinkers should be generalists first, specialists second.

9) "Morality." Ophuls briefly summarizes a fundamental view of many in the environmental movement:

> The crisis of ecological scarcity can be viewed as primarily a moral crisis in which the ugliness and destruction outside us in our environment simply mirror the spiritual wasteland within; the sickness of the earth reflects the sickness in the soul of modern industrial individuals, whose whole lives are given over to gain, to the disease of endless getting and spending that can never satisfy their deeper aspirations and must eventually end in cultural, spiritual, and physical death...the new morality of the steady state must involve a movement from matter toward spirit, not simply in the sense that material pursuits and values will inevitably be de-emphasize and restrained by self-interested necessity, but also in the sense that there will be a recovery or rediscovery of virtue and sanctity. We shall learn again that canons higher than self-interest and individual want are necessary for people to live in productive harmony with themselves and with others.[52]

10) "Post-modernity." "To sum up," Ophuls writes, "ecological scarcity obliges us to abandon most basic modern values in favor of ones that resemble pre-modern values in many important respects." [53]

Ophuls carries this last thought forward in his closing section, crediting at length the British conservative Edmund Burke with a prophetic critique of emergent industrial capitalism and the destruction of community its development has entailed. His 1977 edition contains relatively little on political strategy, other than calling for leadership to help bring about the needed "metanoia" which would make the required political changes possible. In the postscript to the 1992 edition, Ophuls concedes that he has become severely pessimistic about the possibilities of the needed changes being made in a timely manner, and that he had, in 1977, underestimated the holding power of the existing system and its values."...[R]ather than adopt ecological principles for public policy, we seem to do everything we can to avoid facing up to the inevitability of limits and of changing our profligate way of life. In other words, time has grown shorter and the problems have become larger and more entrenched, but our resistance to dealing with them constructively has increased." [54]

Rudolf Bahro. *The Alternative in Eastern Europe*. New York: Schocken Books, 1978. (Published in German, 1977.)

Bahro began his career as a committed East German Marxist who unleashed a powerful critique of East German socialism (from both egalitarian and ecological perspectives), a critique which helped inspire Green political activity in both East and West Germany.

In *The Alternative*, Bahro calls for a "cultural revolution" aimed against "the traditional division of labor," "the exclusion of the many from an education giving them the ability to participate in determining the social synthesis," " the patriarchal model of childhood that restricts development," "lack of community," and "bureaucracy." Bahro proposed four fundamental reforms to help bring these goals about:

First, "The liquidation of bureaucratic corruption from above, in all its open and hidden, sanctioned and unsanctioned forms"; second, "the abolition of piecework and work norms"; third, "the planned periodic participation of the entire managerial and intellectual staff of society in simple operative labor"; and fourth, "a systematic revision of wage-scales according to simple and perceptible criteria...with the aim of taking a decisive step towards just wage relations within the collective worker." [55]

Following these initial steps, the cultural revolution should move on to further goals: to abandon the accumulation of material goods without reference to the "optimalization of conditions of development for fully socialized individuals" (i.e. whether they are good for us); to balance production within the cycles of nature, to reevaluate of the use of time—including not only shorter workweeks but giving "priority for the shortening of psychologically unproductive labor-time within necessary labor-time" (i.e. cutting out unnecessary work); and to reconstruct a culture of both individual initiative and "genuine commonality." Also prominent in Bahro's thought is a full-scale rejection of militarism as practiced in both East and West.

Bahro's thoughts on the relationship between the economy and nature merit further investigation.

If we intend therefore to harmonize man's existence in nature wherever this is possible, than this must lead to a consistent change in the habits of production. The average type of large-scale industry on which the present civilization of the developed countries is based and which is spreading to all other regions, is naturally far removed from being a

technical phenomenon compatible with all forms of society whatsoever.
It has arisen and been constructed on a basis of domination and the
valorization of abstract labor.[56]

The last two sentences represent something of a catechism for serious red-
greens, that is, the notion that exploitation of labor and exploitation of nature
are inextricably linked. Bahro goes on to spell out specific changes that
should be made to push the economy in a green direction including

1) Greater priority on full use and repair of existing capital equipment
   as opposed to building new equipment and buildings;
2) Greater care of existing machinery, more attention to preventive
   maintenance;
3) "Furthest possible reduction of damaging influences on man and
   environment from existing plant and processes, and the absolute
   avoidance of these in new ones";
4) "Stronger macro- and micro-economic measures to reduce the use of
   raw materials and energy";
5) "Orientation towards functionality, solidity (maximum durability)
   and aesthetic quality of mass consumer goods; suspension,
   replacement or substitution of any kind of throwaway product... and
   an end to any kind of 'market-creating' advertising";
6) 100% recycling of waste materials
7) Greater capacity in every community to repair and service existing
   goods.

Taken as a whole, Bahro's agenda "involves renunciation of
'technological leadership' in the sense of capitalist efficiency." [57]

Quite obviously, Bahro's (failed) dream of a new revolutionary
leadership emerging to promote genuine Marxism with a green twist in East
Germany reads rather oddly in the present context. Yet his willingness to
reject both capitalism and actually existing socialism demonstrates the
relevance of his thought to the contemporary debate, particularly when one
observes the close parallels between some of his ideas and those of ecological
writers working within the context of American capitalism. The seven points
noted above are quite demanding requirements, and the structural obstacles
facing them are as serious today as when Bahro forwarded them.

In the years following the publication of *The Alternative*, Bahro moved
sharply away from Marxism into the "fundi" wing of the German Green
movement; during the 1980s Bahro took up the advocacy of "industrial

disarmament," that is the de-industrialization of society, in favor of a return to pre-industrial commune-style ways of life, where communes are given maximum governing powers and with only a minimal state apparatus. (Bahro broke with the German Green Party in 1985 as part of the ongoing ideological conflict between the two wings of that party.) Bahro's program thus shifted, calling for the creation of commune-cells in the midst of industrial society by citizens willing to drop out of the industrial sector and begin building a different way of life. The relationships of the communes to one another politically and economically in Bahro's vision are not clearly spelled out. Indeed, Boris Frankel calls the model "utterly vague" as to specifics, and "industrial disarmament" is probably not an even remotely plausible possibility for the West. Nonetheless, the notion of building up the new institutions (and building blocks for the next stage of development) within the husk of the old society's shell is an important one, with similarities, for instance, to the long-term strategy of building on experiments in community-oriented economics developed by Gar Alperovitz.[58]

Andre Gorz

Capitalism, Socialism, and Ecology. New York: Verso, 1994.
Paths to Paradise. Boston: South End Press, 1985.
Ecology as Politics. Boston: South End Press, 1980.

For over 30 years French radical and ecological thinker Andre Gorz has advocated "utopian" visions based on reshaping the nature of work and reducing overall working hours. Much like Paul and Percival Goodman in *Communitas*, Gorz advocates a bifurcated economy where the basic necessities of life are produced under a centrally planned system in which all citizens would spend part of their time. Through effective use of high technology, Gorz hopes that this "heteronomous" sector will be as small as possible. The rest of the economy would be "free," or autonomous from state compulsion, so that citizens could spend the rest of their time as they wish. To put it another way, Gorz envisions a society working for the good of the community from 9:00 to 11:00 and then having the rest of the day for other endeavors. (Gorz also envisions a third sector of local-level, civil society activity, distinct from the "free" sector.)

At the heart of Gorz's scheme is the notion of workers' self-time management. Workers would be assigned a given number of hours of work to be completed during their working lives (early adulthood until retirement); it would be up to the workers themselves to decide when they wanted to work. Since the lifetime total would be roughly equivalent to working half-time for forty-plus years, many imaginable options would be available, including accelerated work and very early retirement, continual part-time work, sabbatical years, etc. Workers would have access to a guaranteed income separate from their wage earnings.

Gorz is adamant that these reforms alone would be inadequate; what is also needed is a cultural shift and a growth of local community institutions and outlets for democratic participation so that workers would be able to use their newfound freedom of time and security of income in productive ways (not on addictions to consumer pleasures).

> In the current social environment, only work, however ungratifying it may be, offers men and women occasions for association, communication and exchange. The non-work sphere is the sphere of solitude, isolation, enforced idleness for all those who dwell on the periphery and in the suburbs of the great metropolitan agglomerations. Liberated time will be nothing else but empty time unless there are a) a politics of collective equipment which endows communes, cities, or large buildings, with places for meetings, exchange and autonomous activities; b) a politics of cooperation and voluntary association permitting the development, on a local and non-market basis, of all types of collective services...[59]

Gorz's proposed society obviously rejects the goal of economic accumulation for its own sake; the cutback in working hours is the flip side of reducing stress on the environment (a formulation also seen in Schor and Alperovitz).

Gorz's strategy for bringing about the workers' self-managed state remains murky and unconvincing, as the relentless, withering critique of Boris Frankel makes clear. Gorz remains situated within a neo-Marxist framework of social change and looks to a "neo-proletariat" segment of the unemployed and most marginalized workers to be the agent of the needed social change and to make the decisive break with what Gorz terms "productivism." It is not unfair to point out that so far few have signed up for this role.

Lester Milbrath. *Envisioning a Sustainable Society*. Binghamton, NY: SUNY, 1989.

Milbrath's book is another strong effort to spell out the values guiding a "new environmental paradigm," the need for such a paradigm to replace modern industrial-consumer society, and how such change might be brought about. Much of what he has to say regarding such things as agriculture and consumerism is familiar and in line with the Daly and Cobb approach. The focus here is on the specifics of the political-economic system Milbrath believes is necessary.

Milbrath first attempts to separate out "ecological thinking" from both capitalist and socialist ideologies. He asserts that, from a green point of view, the two great systems share many commonalities: anthropocentrism, focus on economic growth, emphasis on hierarchy and the exercise of political power and control, and unbridled pursuit of technology. A new environmental paradigm should reject or modify all of these principles, Milbrath believes. Milbrath then delves into the key issue of the capitalist-socialist debate, ownership of the means of production. Unfortunately perhaps, Milbrath's evenhanded discussion somewhat smooths over the hard consequences of different mixes of ownership and planning. The new environmental paradigm should have both public and private ownership, and "finding the best mixture... requires long experimentation;" [60] Milbrath states that effective democratic or popular control is more important than ownership per se. He concludes that both markets and planning are needed, and that society should seek to balance both cooperative and competitive impulses in human nature.

Milbrath does say that when ecosystem health is at stake, public control, notably of land, is to be preferred, and that too much private ownership can wreck the public welfare. But on the whole, Milbrath's balanced approach avoids taking a firm position on who is to own the economy, leaving doubt as to whether he takes the political consequences of ownership patterns seriously enough.

Milbrath, like Daly and Cobb, endorses the idea of a guaranteed basic income and hopes that a move to more fulfilling work and qualitative human development will be hallmarks of a new environmental paradigm. Milbrath discusses, but stops short of endorsing, "bioregionalism" as a key element of a different paradigm, expressing skepticism about just how self-reliant regions can really become. Milbraith rejects the notion of adjusting political boundaries to ecologically-defined regions, although he allows that bioregional efforts should be welcomed when they spring up.

Movement to a new paradigm requires a long process of "social learning," in Milbrath's view. Writing in 1989, Milbrath predicted at least 20 more years of development along the current "dominator society" path, accompanied by increasing disorientation among the public. Such disorientation inevitably will lead people to look beyond conventional "channels" for fresh ones, and here is where the "new paradigm" has its hope.

Milbrath's emphasis on the importance of ideas and ideological change is noteworthy. Like Ted Trainer (see below), Milbrath believes "sweeping paradigm changes could crystallize within a few months or years," once a critical point of crisis and public awareness has been reached. In the (long) meantime, the task is to encourage social learning by promoting the new paradigm as both an idea and practice. He describes, slightly disturbingly, the early advocates of the new paradigm in almost "chosen people" language: "Those given the gift of understanding will become the conscious mind of the biocommunity, a global mind, that will guide and hasten the transformation." [61]

As a whole, Milbrath's book helps illustrate the conceptual difference between "paradigm" thinking and "system" thinking. Although related and potentially complementary, writers emphasizing "paradigms" tend to focus on values, whereas "system" writers focus on *how exactly concrete institutions could support such values in the real world*, particularly in overcoming the power problems of democracy (the tendency for the affluent and business interests to systematically exercise disproportionate political power). To put the point more sharply, many writers urging a new environmental paradigm are far too tolerant of institutions and power arrangements which undermine the values they urge. The problem is often posed as a matter of changing our discourse and values—which of course it is, in part—with relatively little attention to how to change fundamental power relations in contemporary society (an equally important and even more difficult task).

Herman Daly and John Cobb. *For the Common Good*. Boston: Beacon Press, 1989.

Daly and Cobb spend the first half of their book on an environmental critique of mainstream economics as a discipline and social practice. Among other things, Daly and Cobb pick apart the inadequacy of the GDP as a societal indicator, the one-sided approach to the market and public goods utilized by mainstream economics, and the broader woes of a political and economic culture devoted to "individualism" and material gain at the expense of community well-being. The discussion is solid and informative, if not necessarily novel.

The second part of the book includes eight consecutive chapters suggesting alternative policies to redirect the economy in favor of sustainable communities, followed by two chapters discussing strategy and the role of religion and vision. Taken as a whole the eight chapters strongly suggestive an alternative political-economic architecture, although at no point do Daly and Cobb explicitly speak in the language of "system change" or going beyond capitalism.

1) "Free Trade versus Community." The authors effectively expose the traditional doctrine of comparative advantage, still cited as the basis for free trade ideology, as utterly irrelevant to an era when not only goods but also capital is mobile. Daly and Cobb reject emerging free trade regimes in favor of "balanced trade" aimed at protecting community welfare; they also urge increased effort to make capital less mobile, suggesting that international capital flows would be altogether unnecessary in a "balanced trade" regime.

> We believe it is folly to sacrifice existing institutions of community at the national level in the supposed service of nonexistent institutions of community at the world level. Better to build and strengthen the weakening bonds of national community first, and then expand community by federation into larger trading blocs among national communities that have similar community standards regarding wages, welfare, population control, environmental protection, and conservation. True efficiency lies in the protection of these hard-won community standards from the degenerative competition of individualistic free trade, which comes to rest only at the lowest common denominator.[62]

2) "Population": In order to reduce the total environmental impact of human activity, the authors strongly support population stabilization in the United States. Daly and Cobb favor steps to stem illegal immigration, to

enage motherhood and unwanted babies, and to grant the right of euthanasia to the elderly. For developing countries, Daly and Cobb advocate a "transferable birth quota" plan, first spelled out by Kenneth Boulding, in which each family would have the right to produce 2.1 children; couples wanting more children would have to buy the rights from other families willing to have less than 2. (Each family would be granted 21 "child units," 10 per child, with 1-10th excess.) Aware of the strong and visceral opposition this notion evokes in some, the authors note that "Our proposal is offered as an alternative to the Chinese approach for countries that are both in need of drastic action and capable of implementing it." [63]

3) "Land use": The authors express the goal of increasing wherever possible tracts of wilderness untouched by human activity starting on lands owned by the federal government. Land is to be understood as a "biosphere," not a commodity. Rangeland with cattle should revert to wilderness, inefficient farmland using large amounts of irrigated water should revert to range, etc. "A balanced reduction of both rangeland and cropland would hardly be noticeable in the supermarket," state the authors, who go on to contend that "Half or more of the land area of the United States could be freed from human settlement, agriculture, and the grazing of domesticated animals." [64]

In terms of urban land, the authors focus on the need to move land from "commodity to trust." They endorse Henry George's concept of taxing land value increases in order to return the "unearned increment" to the community and simultaneously reduce taxes on productive activities. This is part and parcel of a broader philosophy of taxing "bads," not "goods." They also suggest that outright community ownership of land would be appropriate in some cases; such ownership "would give maximum freedom for planning patterns of healthy development." [65]

The authors also suggest a policy of limiting mineral extraction (including oil) from land to just 2% of proven reserves annually. This would effect some mineral markets not at all, yet lead to ecologically appropriate price increases reflecting the current overuse of some scarce minerals (namely oil!) Such a policy would in turn stimulate drastic improvements in energy efficiency, saving the society more money. Finally, the authors propose replanning human settlements to minimize energy and resource use. Daly and Cobb support the notion of significant population decentralization, both by moving urban populations to strengthened rural communities and small towns, and by consciously planning towns connected to urban centers by public transportation, not highway-fed suburban sprawl. They also discuss favorably Paolo Soleri's 1969 proposal for arcologies—remarkably compact, fully integrated urban living units contained under a single roof.

4) "Agriculture": The authors spell out the common green critique of American agricultural practices, pointing to the prodigious use of oil and water resources, which makes American agriculture hugely productive in terms of dollar input-output, but also hugely wasteful in terms of *resource* input-output. Daly and Cobb urge a return to smaller farms that utilize more human labor and solar energy in place of natural resource inputs, stating that farms as small as 440 acres could achieve the economies of scale needed for mechanized farming.

They also draw attention to the dying out of rural American communities, seeing the health of the "family farm" as vitally important to regional self-sufficiency and ecological sustainability. Policies that explicitly support family farms (and reasonable land prices), heavily penalize agricultural polluters, and remove present subsidies that encourage wasteful practices, are crucial steps, say the authors, to the larger goal of much more localized agricultural production.

5) "Industry": The authors repeat their call for the United States to withdraw from the free trading system. The most interesting suggestion in this chapter is the idea of "regional decentralization." Noting that capital mobility *within* the United States also destabilizes local communities, creates social costs, and strengthens corporate management's hand vis-a-vis labor, Daly and Cobb urge a "regionalization of economic power and activity that would attach capital to regions." [66] To this end, they propose "the breakup of conglomerates," call for local buy-outs of plants scheduled for closing (noting that "sales to workers are an ideal solution"), and advocate giving local communities right-of-first-refusal on any sale of plants, promoting community and regionally-made products, and integrating the interests of business and labor in local decisionmaking. The overall goal is substantial "economic self-determination" for states and cities.

6) "Labor": Daly and Cobb are for worker ownership when possible, the rehumanization of the work place, and full employment policies (including shortened work weeks to help bring this about).

7) "Income policies and taxes": The authors propose a guaranteed subsistence income for all, based on the model of Milton Friedman's negative income tax, estimated at roughly 9,000 1989 dollars, to be financed out of an income tax rate of 50% (with exemptions for charities, small political donations, job-related expenses such as child care, and home improvements). At the same time, the authors would end corporate taxation, require all

profits to be distributed to stockholders as income, and count on increased revenues from tariffs, taxes on pollution, and the use of scarce natural resources.

The authors also believe that a 50% income tax, combined with effective inheritance and gift taxes, can limit intergenerational transfers of large wealth. In a healthy community, they add, the idea of income maximums as well as income minimums, perhaps at a ratio of 10 to 1, might be desirable, although they do not fully endorse the idea. "We hope that over the years a combination of income and inheritance taxes, on the one hand, and social dividends, worker ownership of businesses, and guaranteed employment on the other, will reduce the spread of incomes from their present exaggerated range. The goal for an economics of community is not equality, but limited inequality." [67]

8) "National Security": This chapter is essentially a critique of Cold War-level military spending, with an emphasis on non-military threats to national security including environmental decay, economic decline, loss of national morale, and so forth.

In terms of how to get from here to there, the authors suggest five obvious loci of needed change: the university and educational practices (towards green education); rebuilding local communities *as communities*; changing trade policies; replacing the GNP with alternative measures of well-being; and changing public attitudes.

In their final, more personal chapter, they discuss the relationship of these fundamental changes to a religious vision, suggesting that theism is helpful in checking idolatry (the market), transcending narrow self-interest (community), and in eliciting the personal commitments needed to bring about change.

On the whole, Daly and Cobb have spelled out the desirable values and goals of the "sustainable development" movement to an impressive degree: less emphasis on economic growth, strengthened local communities, no NAFTA/GATT, reduced capital mobility, promotion of worker ownership, reduced scale of government and economy, and the elimination of a wide range of ecological inefficiencies from land use to resource depletion. The shortcomings of the book lie only in its avoidance of the hard political obstacles to achieving their goals via reform. Simply put, the authors do not locate their vision within a serious analysis of capitalist power relations, nor do they locate the likely social actors on behalf of such a vision or an identifiable process whereby such sweeping changes as they hope for might move from the margins to center stage. Moreover, the specific institutional architecture Daly and Cobb endorse—small businesses, worker-owned when possible—is subject to critique on the grounds that under market processes such firms will inevitably grow and replicate modern-style corporations. Still, Daly and Cobb have articulated an admirable, coherent public philosophy of community-oriented ecological economics; the problem is the massive array of political power opposed to their agenda.

Hazel Henderson. *Building a Win-Win World.* San Francisco: Barret Koelher, 1996.

In a series of books (and a large volume of op-eds and shorter papers) dating back to *The Politics of the Solar Age* (1980), Henderson has been at the forefront in proposing alternative measures of well-being to economic growth. Henderson has devised a set of alternative indicators (as have Daly and Cobb in collaboration with Clifford Cobb), taking account of use of nonrenewable resources, pollution, and various standard quality of life measures such as crime rates and health statistics to provide a more meaningful measure of progress in American society. At the same time, Henderson has often critiqued the scarcity assumptions of conventional economics and emphasized the need to make economic decisions that are driven by values, rather than let values be driven by economics.

The political strategy implicit in the (rapidly maturing) alternative indicators movement is that by "shifting the bottom line" of public attention away from such abstractions as GDP growth to a richer set of indicators, greater public attention will be focused on real problems such as pollution and the time squeeze. A near-term goal, for instance, would be for the network news to announce indicators of our declining ecological health in addition to the standard growth numbers. The theory seems to be that lack of knowledge or factual command by the public of "what's really going on" is the chief obstacle to better policy formulation. This idea seems highly dubious (if unobjectionable in itself) as a political strategy. The nature of discourse carried out among elite opinion makers, however, might indeed be altered (probably not seismically) if more attention were placed on alternative indicators. And it is also the case that a genuine sustainable society *would* need such indicators to help in policymaking and in evaluating political alternatives. The indicators movement is thus a useful contribution, but quite limited in itself as a tool for changing the society in a more than marginal manner.

Douglas Booth

Regional Long Waves, Uneven Development, and the Cooperative Alternative. New York: Praeger, 1987.

"Economic Democracy as an Environmental Measure," *Ecological Economics*, 1995, Vol. 12.

Review of Daly and Cobb's *For the Common Good* in *Review of Social Economy*, Summer 1994.

Booth's review of Daly and Cobb makes crystal clear a fundamental point: Achieving a steady-state economy is inconsistent with maintaining growth-oriented corporate institutions. Booth, in previous work, has explored this question further, suggesting that cooperatives show strong promise as the basis for a more stable and more just economy that might, possibly, also be more consistent with a steady-state economic regime.

Booth's argument here is straightforward: worker cooperatives logically prefer to focus on minimizing the cost of nonlabor inputs, whereas capitalist firms in some circumstances find it easier to maximize exploitation of labor instead of pursuing efficiencies in nonlabor inputs. This means that cooperatives should be more efficient in their use of energy, materials, and other resources than capitalist firms. Booth garners empirical evidence to support this claim from cooperatives operating in several capitalist countries, including the Pacific Northwest's plywood cooperatives and the Mondragon system.

Unlike capitalist firms, worker cooperatives also offer a natural limit on growth; Booth argues that coops will grow "to the point where per worker income is maximized," but no farther. Yet, in many observed cooperatives, growth rates are in fact faster than in conventional firms (especially where an adequate supply of capital is available to support such growth). Indeed, this fact has been one of the prime arguments of economist advocates of the worker-owned firm who emphasize its job-creating potential. Booth's answer to this point is that rapidly growing coops are an artifact of an economy operating at less-than-full employment; in a region facing severe unemployment, such as Basque in the mid-50s where Mondragon was begun, it is natural that growth and job creation become primary social objectives for cooperatives. In contrast, in a full-employment economy, other priorities could emerge. Importantly (and related to Schweickart's proposal), in a regime in which worker firms depended upon provision of external capital for expansion, such capital could be constrained or expanded to slow or accelerate growth.

Booth ends his paper by admitting that much more research is needed to determine the extent to which worker-owned firms can improve ecological outcomes, whether as separate units operating within a largely capitalist system or in a regime where cooperatives are the primary economic unit. For a critique of the notion that the worker cooperative model can serve as a primary basis for an ecologically sustainable system, see the Schweickart annotation in chapter two.

Juliet Schor

The Unexpected Decline of Leisure. New York: Basic Books, 1991.
A Sustainable Economy for the 21st Century. Westfield, NJ: Open Media. 1995.

Schor is best known for her book documenting long trends towards increased working hours in the United States. (Other data collected by John Robinson of the University of Maryland actually differ with Schor's conclusions, although Robinson himself agrees that many Americans subjectively experience a time squeeze in their own lives.) Not surprisingly, then, the reduction of working hours (by as much as one-half), and an acceptance of less growth in the consumption of goods form the centerpiece of Schor's vision of a sustainable economy.

Other work by Schor on consumption has demonstrated that for many consumer goods in the present economy—most famously, lipstick—the status value of the good, not its intrinsic use value, plays a major role in shaping consumer behavior. This finding suggests that in a society where invidious comparisons of status were less important, part of the impulse to consume would vanish; alternatively, sumptuary laws (such as the mandatory provision of school uniforms) also might rein in particular forms of socially irrational overconsumption.

In collaboration with the New Party, Schor's pamphlet "A Sustainable Economy for the 21st Century" attempts to spell out for a popular audience an economic policy agenda, an "optimistic economic vision," worthy of widespread support. Unlike most of the theorists reviewed here, Schor makes the claim that the New Party agenda is attuned to the actual desires of American public opinion who want a cleaner environment, more free time, fairness and equity, and better quality of life—values which contradict the ongoing trends of "global capitalism." In this vein, the values of the New Party agenda are stated as "sustainability, democratic control, equality, and efficiency."

As to the time squeeze, Schor's central proposal is to require employers to allow workers, if they choose, to take increased productivity in the form of shorter work weeks, not higher pay. (Schor cites poll data stating that if Americans were financially secure, only 23 per cent of adults would choose to work full-time.) Three problems with this proposal immediately emerge, given the context of a capitalist political economy: First, in recent years productivity growth has not automatically translated into wage growth, so there may be no choice between more wages and more time to be made (although this situation would probably be corrected if unions were stronger). Second, the cost of adding workers to make up for the lost production when workers cut their own work weeks, including the costs of hiring, training, and managing, as well as payroll taxes, would probably inspire considerable resistance among employers. Third, this strategy would distribute more free time among workers in a highly unequal manner. Workers in industries experiencing high productivity growth could cut their hours substantially, while workers in service sectors would have little opportunity to cut work weeks.

All these points suggest that an effective move to shorter work weeks for all would have to be a society-wide social choice, not a product of wage bargaining agreements. Thus, governments might pass laws cutting the standard workweek and requiring businesses to pay overtime to those who work longer than 35 hours, a measure which, combined with reduced payroll taxes, might provide sufficient incentive for employers to add jobs while cutting hours; this reduction could be implemented gradually over a five year period in lieu of wage increases. Alternatively, or ideally as a complement to the above strategy, enterprises directly controlled by the community or by its workers would naturally have a stronger incentive to choose shorter hours and lower profits. If such enterprises were assured of an ongoing, stable market, then it might be possible to evade the "grow-or-die" dynamic common in capitalist enterprises, and translate success into shorter working hours, not market expansion.

Other specific proposals of the New Party economic agenda:

- Providing subsidies for job creation and local government direct employment programs to combat unemployment

- Readjusting the GNP to include natural resource accounting and instituting a "green tax" on consumers
- Instituting industry-wide environmental standards to eliminate competitive pressures towards wasteful packaging and other ecologically harmful practices
- Increasing investments in public transportation and support for new forms of community design based on mixed land-use patterns
- Providing government assistance to democratic economic enterprises, including coops, worker-owned firms, and community enterprise
- Mandating representation on corporate boards from "stakeholder groups"
- Reviving union membership and encouraging the development of less hierarchical forms of management
- Raising the minimum wage sharply and providing basic income grants to all citizens as a matter of right
- Upgrading public schools through federal investments
- Implementing principles of "fair trade"

The document as a whole thus represents a wide array of the ideas expressed in this bibliography, yet the precise path to institutional change along these lines remain unclear, largely because the bulk of the New Party's most dramatic proposals depend on far-off national-level reforms. What is missing from this document is a sense of how specific communities might begin implementing large portions of the overall vision (including the reduction of working hours) even in the absence of national-level reform, and how stronger public support for the larger-scale institutional change ultimately needed might be built.

Ted Trainer

The Conserver Society. London: Zed Books, 1995.
Towards a Sustainable Economy. Oxford: Jon Carpenter, 1996.

Trainer provides a brief but stinging critique of the ecological consequences of modern consumer society, then goes on to sketch an agenda for not so much an alternative political system as an alternative civilization, based on minimizing ecological impacts. The changes proposed are profound—more radical in scope, though of the same general tenor as Daly and Cobb—and again fall into eight different sectors.

The most fundamental change, Trainer states, is in the required economic system of a conserver society: "There is no possibility whatsoever of achieving a sustainable society while we have anything like the present economic system...The problems are primarily due to over-production, overconsumption and over-development and it is our economic system which inevitably leads to these outcomes." [68] Trainer's critique of capitalism rests less on social justice concerns or Marxist analysis than on the proposition that the scale of the present growth-driven economy is already far bigger than what our ecosystems can handle. However, Trainer does also cite unemployment, waste, inequality, and inappropriate development as evidence of capitalism's failings.

"The essential theme in the new economic order must be the development of many small-scale local and regional economies that are largely self-sufficient." Trainer would start at the lowest level possible, advocating significant household self-production of food, with the more immediate goal of maximizing local food production at the neighborhood and town levels. This pattern would extend to other areas of the economy. "Most of the goods and services we need could easily come from within 2 to 3 km of where we live, i.e. from within our town or suburb," [69] the author claims, including health care, food, water ("from rooftops and tanks"), sewage (Recycled to local food production), composted garbage, energy (from renewable sources nearby and solar-passive design), housing materials, timber, pottery, clothing ("much produced and repaired within the household"), shoes, furniture, leisure, and finance. (There would be no need for big finance in Trainer's system, only, at most, small-scale localized banking.) Trainer acknowledges the need for some trade between regions for such things as appliances, transport, capital equipment, etc, but emphasizes that cities of 10-50,000 people should be able to be largely self-reliant.

At the national level, focusing on Australia, Trainer, like Daly and Cobb, advocates delinking from the global economy. "Either you make sure your basic economy is protected from the ravages of foreign competition, or you see it largely taken over or wiped out by the most powerful players—a few giant foreign corporations and banks." [70] Trainer acknowledges that protectionism will involve higher prices for consumers, but sees this as a small cost to pay for stabilizing local economies and communities.

As to ownership regime, Trainer is for a mixed economy, but one dominated by community ownership. Trainer envisions "much community property and many community functions, such as the orchards, the windmill, the workshops and many cooperative 'firms' producing basic goods and services," as well as a crucial role for community development corporations, community loan funds, community land trusts, etc. Trainer does allow for some free-enterprise business on the model of "the corner shop or the small firm owned and run by those who work in it," that is, businesses anchored in community that have little incentive to expand markets. Trainer also wishes to see a strong increase in the barter economy and local currencies, and work for cash reduced to one day a week.

Trainer acknowledges that "the basic economic issues must be settled via some form of social planning," at the level of the national state when necessary, but at the local level as much as possible (citing the kibbutz as a model). Capitalist-style, large-scale financial institutions would be banned in favor of small community banks holding savings; eventually, Trainer envisions an end to loans at interest. Simply put, in a no-growth economy communities will only rarely need large sums of capital. Indeed, Trainer feels the goal for the immediate future should be to shrink the size of the economy.

Coupled with these changes would be a radical reduction in work weeks and a reshifting of job responsibilities, giving each citizen a wider variety of tasks and job experiences.

Trainer carries out analyses of the food, energy, housing, and water sectors illuminated by the basic principles noted above: local self-production and reduction of resource use whenever possible. Trainer is particularly adamant about the need for Westerners to accept less in the way of luxury consumer goods, and he frequently contrasts Western affluence to Third World poverty (and assumes a direct causal relationship between the two), going so far as to say "we must come to understand...that luxuries are disgusting and murderous." [71]

Besides his thoughts about the economy, the most unconventional part of Trainer's analysis is his proposed redesign of human settlements to minimize transportation needs, maximize room for nature, and reduce overall human impact. Trainer urges much smaller communities (including smaller neighborhoods within existing cities), no wastage of land, and a rollback of the impact of the automobile.

As Trainer notes in the conclusion, his book indeed leaves "no doubt that the alternatives are there," and that "there is nothing to stop us from implementing them on a large scale—except the will to do so." [72] Still, Trainer has an appropriate sobriety regarding prospects for change, stating that a long process of reconstruction, 20 years or perhaps longer, will be needed, until a breaking point is reached and rapid change becomes possible (on the Berlin Wall model). And, he concedes, the envisioned changes may well be impossible—but he takes heart from the rise of an anti-consumerism mentality in the past 30 years and poll data from Ronald Inglehart suggesting a steady rise in "postmaterialist" values since 1970.

Changing one's personal lifestyle, joining an existing political group, or even joining a green party are all useful acts but in the end inadequate to the task, Trainer says. It is far better to begin the immediate work of rebuilding local community, and he provides over a dozen suggestions on how to do so (such as start a community garden, organize a cooperative, plant permaculture, draw up plans for alternative community design, etc.). Such action, Trainer supposes, will create more and more opportunities for persons to productively drop out of mainstream consumer society, give up a full time job, reduce consumption, and at the same time build up the concrete basis of an alternative community with alternative values, eventually pushing to change local and then national governmental policies. Trainer also compares his ideas to traditional Marxist conceptions; in the end he rejects, tentatively, the notion of a revolutionary (authoritarian) leadership to push people to the needed changes. Instead, he allies himself with a prototypical anarchist view of participation from below as the means for effecting systemic change.

David Pepper

The Modern Environmental Movement. London: Routledge, 1996.
Eco-socialism. London: Routledge, 1993.

One of the foremost voices from a "red-green" perspective in Great Britain today, Pepper has written extensively on what programmatic responses the environmental movement should undertake. These books provide a fine overview of the debate and tensions among various strands of the environmental movement, from those who believe "inner consciousness" will be the ultimate source of change to full-blown materialists, who, following the classic Marxian base-superstructure formulation, hold that attitudinal change towards nature can only follow changes in the structure of production. Pepper allies himself more closely with the latter view. He is hostile to green critiques of "anthropocentrism," as well as Gaia-age ecological thought that focuses on spirituality as an agent of change, and is respectful yet skeptical of anarchist-inspired notions of social change. In particular, Pepper sees the notion of building communities that "prefigure" the desired society to come, as emphasized to some extent by Trainer and especially Murray Bookchin, as an inadequate model of social change.

To Pepper, the "socialist" content of "eco-socialism" must be taken seriously: capital must be met head on in a power confrontation, and the fundamental production relationships of capitalism must change. For this reason, Pepper, far more than most ecologically-minded writers, stakes hope on existing labor organizations, to be reawakened as an environmentally-minded movement, as an agent to challenge an ecologically destructive capitalism. (Such a far-sighted leadership role for unions is extremely difficult to imagine in America, where it has taken considerable upheaval and struggle to get the national labor leadership to simply advocate the point that "America deserves a raise" and to finally put substantial resources into new organizing.) Pepper also effectively insists that developing an ecologically sustainable regime must involve the use of state power and planning; the alternatives, reverting to autarkic, locally-based production, or relying on some form of market, are unworkable in one case and undesirable in the other, at least as the basis for an entire system.

Pepper's approach seeks to cast "environmental issues" as widely as possible (vehicle pollution, street violence, unemployment, "loss of community and access to countryside") so as to speak to the concrete needs of the majority of citizens, especially those in urban areas who can be more easily organized and tend to be more sympathetic to progressive politics. While the ultimate goal should be to capture state power, Pepper appreciates the need for intermediate efforts to put eco-socialism into practice as a counter-example.

In this regard, Pepper, criticizes recent trends in the Mondragon cooperatives, but nonetheless holds hope for the idea of alternative production that combines worker control with ecological criteria. As an example of what might be possible, he cites the 1976 Lucas Aerospace Combine Shop Stewards Committee plan, formulated by workers at a British defense contractor, to redirect production from defense to ecologically minded products, such as alternative energy projects. Pepper also endorses "municipal socialism," referring to both city control of productive capital and government efforts to upgrade the physical environment of urban areas. Pepper sees the city level as the appropriate scale for public expenditure to create jobs in environmentally helpful activities, such as alternative energy, tree planting, and the establishment of parks and horticulture sites. Finally, Pepper notes that conventional "anarchist/utopian" ecological ideas such as alternative currencies ought to be supported by "eco-socialists," even though such approaches cannot directly challenge capital.

Curiously, Pepper is unclear as to what the larger outcome of his hoped-for confrontation with capital will be. Nationalization of industries? Decentralized municipal control of industry combined with state-wide planning? Some form of direct worker control? While Pepper clearly believes in a strong state, extensive planning, and probably some form of market mechanism, the larger institutional framework of his "eco-socialism" remains to be fleshed out. Particularly glaring is his lack of discussion on the time and work week question. Still, Pepper does successfully navigate through the main currents of ecological thought on both sides of the Atlantic in these two books, providing powerful arguments as to why a pure "small is beautiful" approach needs to be fused with elements of traditional left-wing politics in forging an alternative to contemporary capitalism.

Larry Rasmussen. *Earth Community, Earth Ethics*. Maryknoll, NY: Orbis Books, 1996.

Attention to the consequences of fundamental assumptions —cosmologies, as it were—is the overarching theme of Rasmussen's weighty volume, *Earth Ethics, Earth Community*. The book makes at least three significant contributions to the discourse of ecological ethics and the question of what a just, ecologically sound social order looks like. First, in undertaking an "Earth Scan" to track the nature of the collision course between present economic systems and ecosystem health, Rasmussen provides a veritable source book of recent scientific, policy, and ethical literature pertaining to ecosystems and ecological health. Second, growing out of his personal involvement with the World Council of Churches' sustainability efforts, Rasmussen presents a skilled critique of prevailing notions of "sustainable development" which presume to graft good, green ideas onto the fundaments of a corporate, global economy in a top-down process, and instead upholds the very different notion of "sustainable community." (Subsequent to the book's publication, Rasmussen has stated that the term "sustainable community" must be used with caution, noting that the term seems to validate, wrongly, the notion of a static state of affairs as the goal of ecological economics.) Third, Rasmussen broaches the question of how to reformulate "cosmologies"—overall ethical frames—from a variety of theological angles in a series of largely discrete, homiletic chapters in the second half of the book. Each of these contributions will be examined in turn.

Rasmussen's "Earth Scan" first locates the brief period of rapid human economic expansion and industrial growth as a violent blip in the context of the "slow womb" of Earth's five billion year development. The point of this exercise is to lift the reader out of the relentless anthropocentric frame of current ethical discourse, including much of the discourse pertaining to "environmental issues." Rasmussen carries the story from primordial beginnings through the industrial revolution to the present ecological-economic-political regime which he terms "environmental apartheid," connoting not only the wildly disproportionate distribution of economic and ecological harms among racial and class groups in contemporary capitalism, but also the assumed (and realized) separation between the interests of humanity and the well-being of nature. The intent here is to push not only for good empirical analysis of existing trends, but to illustrate a holistic frame of ethical analysis which acknowledges that human-earth problems are at least as important, ethically, as the human-to-human problems that generally occupy center stage in North American Christian ethics.

Part one of the book also contains Rasmussen's discussion of ecological economics and "sustainable development," and hence the "policy" core of the overall argument. Rasmussen describes our present economy as one whose "plimsoll line is missing." That is to say, we have no measure (or seemingly even concern with) judging when the impact of our economic activities are overwhelming and "overshooting" nature's "carrying capacity."

Rasmussen then pushes the discussion beyond this increasingly common ecological critique of "cowboy capitalism." Also inadequate, in Rasmussen's view, are top-down models for creating ecologically sustainable economies, be it the once-ascendant "planetary management" model of "Spaceship Earth" favored by former EPA Administrator William Clark, which presumes that human beings are capable of perfectly intelligent and rational management of something so complex as the health of the natural world, or the "sustainable development" lingo which has come to the fore in recent years. The problem with the "sustainable development" paradigm, as best illustrated in the landmark Brundtland Commission Report of 1991, is that it seeks to correct and temper, not fundamentally challenge, the institutional bases and presumptions guiding growth economics worldwide. To wit, the fundamental premise that the purpose of the economy is to increase consumption—not support human beings equitably, sustain communities, or preserve ecosystems—is left intact. What is left is to try to place as green a face as possible on a system dynamics that fundamentally undermines the goals of a socially just ecological sustainability. While Rasmussen rightly concedes that there is considerable room for tangible short-run improvement by moving in this direction, he urges that a longer-term solution requires a different framework, namely, the notion of "sustainable community." Sustainable community starts with the "*oikos*" (household) and its needs as the primary unit of consideration, with community health, equitable distribution of resources, meaningful work, and the sustainable use of resources as building blocks, not afterthoughts.

Part Two turns to the question of how to conceptualize an "Earth Faith" that expresses a theological understanding of humans, not as masters of nature, but as embedded in a divine creation which has value beyond human beings. While there is a certain logic to the progression of these chapters, the discussion of "Earth Faith" is not a linear, discursive argument, but an attempt to cover numerous dimensions of the cosmological issue. Rasmussen is ultimately pushing in these chapters towards "an evolutionary sacramental cosmology"—that is, a world view emphasizing the divine aspect of all creation, yet without identifying "the creaturely" as God—that embraces both an "earthly asceticism" and prophetic efforts to liberate life. The most sustained theological argumentation is given to Rasmussen's distinctions between "dominion," "steward," and "partnership" models of humanity's relationship to nature. Parallel to Rasmussen's treatment of "cowboy economics," "sustainable development," and "sustainable community," the author clearly rejects the dominion conception, praises aspects of but does not embrace the stewardship model, and leans towards adoption of the still-in-formation "partnership" notion. This last concept recognizes that "whatever power we wield as a species, we do not legislate the laws of an encompassing nature" and points towards "the revival of a creation loving asceticism" that "loves earth fiercely in a simple way of life."

Rasmussen closes with a brief review of the notion of sustainable community and a listing of some helpful, on-the-ground alternative practices which point towards sustainable community, such as ecologically sensitive industrial planning in Kalundborg, Denmark, the Swedish Natural Step network that is pushing for ambitious reductions in waste and ecological damage, and the burgeoning community-supported agriculture movement in the United States.

Rasmussen's final point is that given the enormity of the task of rebuilding the world, a vital religious faith provides the needed capacity to replenish vitality, refresh minds, and restore hope. Rasmussen urges that

114

without "faith stories," there is little basis for challenging the dominant cosmological frame of nature-for-human-use, much less stepping up to the task of "the regular renewal of moral-spiritual and sociopsychological energy in a long season of forced society-nature experimentation"—even as more and more of a "beloved world" is extinguished with another day's loss of rainforest acres.[73]

Murray Bookchin. *From Urbanization to Cities.* New York: Cassell, 1992.

Bookchin, author of over a dozen books on social theory, is credited as the leading intellectual proponent of "social ecology" and as a guiding light of the anarchistic wing of green thought. The essence of social ecology is the integration of ecology with political and social reconstruction: the route to a sustainable world must run through the creation of a different kind of politics, polity, and citizenry. Bookchin's political philosophy is one of "confederal municipalism," based on local polities governed by face-to-face democracy that exercises real power over social and economic decision making. *From Urbanization to Citizenship* presents an extended argument for "confederal municipalism."

Bookchin's concern is not how to institute a holistic full-blown systemic alternative to capitalism; rather he argues as strenuously as possible for a particular view of what the fundamental building block of such a system must be. Bookchin puts this vision in succinct terms: "The recovery and development of politics must, I submit, take its point of departure from the citizen and his or her immediate environment beyond the familial and private areas of life. There can be no politics without community. And by community I mean a municipal association of people reinforced by its own economic power, its own institutionalization of the grass roots, and the confederal support of nearby communities organized into a territorial network on a local and regional scale." [74] Bookchin states that such municipal "recovery" of politics can take place in any size city, but also states that a long-term goal of his public philosophy would be to physically decentralize urban megalopolises.

Bookchin is not vague in stating what the core economic institution of a revived "libertarian municipalism" must be: municipally-owned enterprise, which Bookchin contrasts in the strongest possible terms to both large-scale state enterprise and worker management of firms. (He describes the latter as a "blatant bourgeois trick," noting that "the effective use of 'workers' participation' in production, even the outright handing over of industrial operations to the workers who perform them, has become another form of time-studies, assembly-line rationalization, another form of the systematic abuse of labor, by bringing labor itself into complicity with its own exploitation." [75])

Bookchin catalogues the advantages of municipal enterprise as follows:

1) Municipal enterprise politicizes economic life and makes possible transparent, democratic decision making about production. "The economy would cease to be merely an economy in the conventional sense of the term, composed of capitalistic, nationalized, or 'worker-controlled' enterprises. The municipality, more precisely the citizen body in face-to-face assembly, would absorb the economy into its public business, divesting it of a separate identity that can become privatized into a self-serving enterprise." [76]

2) As contrasted to syndicalist conceptions, with municipal enterprises there is no inherent conflict between producer factions and the community as a whole.

3) Bookchin thinks that even "vocational identities" can be made subordinate to one's identity as a citizen, since city workers must deliberate on economic decision making in an open forum.

4) Direct local control of economic life would make possible alternative economic arrangements: Bookchin suggests different forms of distribution arrangements, and hints that "freedom from the factory" for workers—more free time—would become possible.

As for ecological problems, Bookchin clearly believes this structure will make visible the ecological consequences of production and give communities incentive to develop environmentally sound habits. He further states that developing an ecological society must mean getting literally to the root of the problem: "For those who rightly call for a new technology, new sources, of energy, new means of transportation, and new ecological lifeways, can a new society be anything less than a Community of communities based on confederation rather than statism?" [77]

Powerful as this vision is, it is also the case that Bookchin's conception of "confederal municipalism" does not address several key questions: Is it really desirable—or feasible—to municipalize all economic activity, as Bookchin implies? What is to be done about forms of industrial production, such as airplanes and superconductors, which intrinsically require large scale? Is face-to-face democracy a live option in medium and large-scaled communities? Need all decisions be made democratically, or is it drastically

116

more efficient for society to allow permanent government officials to make some decisions? How, ultimately, will the confederal municipalist strategy confront centralized forms of capitalist power, specifically the corporation? Bookchin's powerful case for municipal enterprise as the economic building block of a new society is diluted by his failure to address these key questions of feasibility—and institutional design—in a convincing fashion.

Gar Alperovitz

Twentieth Century Systems—and Beyond (forthcoming manuscript).

"Sustainability and the System Problem," *PEGS Journal*, Spring 1996.

"Beyond Socialism and Capitalism," in Hartman and Vilanova, eds. *Paradigms Lost*. London: Pluto Press, 1990.

"Speculative Theory and Regime Alternatives," in Soltan and Elkin, eds. *The Constitution of Good Societies*. University Park, PA: The Pennsylvania State University Press, 1996.

"Building a Living Democracy," *Sojourners*, July 1990.

"Distributing our Technological Inheritance," *Technology Review*, October 1994.

"Notes Toward a Pluralist Commonwealth," in Alperovitz and Staughton Lynd, *Strategy and Program*. Boston: Beacon Press, 1973.

"The Reconstruction of Community Meaning," *Tikkun*, May/June 1996.

Alperovitz's work qualifies as a community-based counter to "market socialism" and as a serious attempt to specify the institutional requirements of an ecologically sustainable society, paying far more attention to this question than is the case with most market socialist writers. Alperovitz also is centrally concerned with the institutional requirements of meaningful democratic governance, with particular emphasis on "equality" as a precondition of strong democracy. Thus, while the following discussion takes ecological concern as the starting point, the model itself seeks to meld insights from political theory, political economy, and ecological economics into a comprehensive vision.

According to Alperovitz, there are (at least) four fundamental structural problems in capitalism which militate against ecological sustainability:

First, the ability of private firms to pass social costs (i.e .pollution) off on to the community;

Second, the overall growth trajectory of the system;

Third, the capacity of interest groups representing corporate power to block or dampen "reform" efforts, most spectacularly in the case of efficient use of technology (compare subsidies of the nuclear vs. solar industries, or the auto vs. rail industries);

Fourth, the fact of economic insecurity at the individual, community, and firm levels which compels all actors to acquire "more" as soon as possible, because one may not have any tomorrow, or because if one does not climb the ladder (or increase market share) they may fall down (or *lose* market share).

The following discussion proceeds by discussing Alperovitz's structural solution to the first, third, and fourth problems, followed by additional comments that flesh out his overall vision. After this, a possible answer to the difficult second problem emerges. This annotation concludes with a summary of Alperovitz's proposed strategy.

Problem #1: For Alperovitz, a structural solution to the first problem requires that firms must be able to "internalize" the externalities; functionally, this means that they should be significantly community owned, or owned by some combination of interests guaranteeing a strong community stake (worker-community joint interest, partial ownership in locally-owned firms, and so forth). Under a community ownership regime, if a community wishes to pollute its own air, it can make the decision to do so; or it might decide not to pollute itself and instead accept a lower profit margin. The key point is that the community, in a democratic process, has the power to determine the ecological behavior of its major industry. Obviously, a problem emerges when one considers emissions into the air which might pollute someone else; a macro-level planning capacity beyond the micro-level community-ownership structure is required, as noted below.

Problem #3: This is the "power problem of democracy"; Alperovitz's answer runs on several lines. First, the core structure of community-owned industry might negate some of the disproportionate power of industry over decision-making, especially at the local level. Second, a regime of greater equality in which democratic capacities for participation have been truly broadened to include each and all would undercut differences in political influence that result from unequal resources and time. Third, the breakdown of federal power into regional units should make for more coherent, responsive policy-making and, again, should dampen the power of concentrated vested interests; social scientists studying regimes built on strong public cooperation (such as some West European social democracies) emphasize the importance of smaller scale in making a workable public consensus possible. Fourth, a different culture, rooted in the local-level experience of ecological responsibility developed slowly over time through community ownership and stewardship, is seen as trickling *up* to provide steering values (norms) to the larger scale decisions (rail vs. road, fossil fuels vs. solar, etc.).

Problem #4: To counter the insecurity-striving-for-growth dynamic, the author envisions planning to provide at least partial security to individuals, communities, and their firms. Taking a cue from the current Earned Income Tax Credit and social dividend strategies abroad, individuals would receive, by virtue of their membership in the community, payments from "community inheritance trust funds," probably managed at the federal level. (While considerable accumulation within one's lifetime would be allowed, apart from a modest allowance for bequests to children, the bulk of these estates would be placed upon death into a community trust fund in recognition of the central role of the community as a whole in creating wealth.) A secure stream of (partial) income is seen as important not only to equality but to liberty.

Providing economic stability for communities would require two kinds of planning mechanisms. First, at the local level, the challenge would be to stabilize, say, 40,000 jobs in a town of 100,000. Outright community ownership and other public jobs need only comprise some 15,000 of these jobs—spinoffs from spending generated by these core jobs would naturally create the other 25,000 jobs—provided there is a sufficient level of local buying in the economy to maximally re-circulate the money. Hence, in most cases a program of local import substitution would be appropriate.

Second, the question arises as to the stability of community firms operating in the larger market. Long term contracts between community firms to buy from each other (as is often present between suppliers and corporations presently) would help each firm plan long term and partially guarantee their market. Then, in the event of firm decline, or a need to shift to a different product due to changing market conditions, there would have to be a regional-level mechanism to provide funds to retool the town's capital equipment and convert to a different product or industry. The town would not be allowed to die—not only is this extremely wasteful of accumulated public capital and investment, it is very much the fear of death which currently drives towns to pursue growth-at-all costs strategies (often selling out lock, stock, and barrel to corporations who agree to move in town).

Although a long term evolutionary path is envisioned, the following seven points sum up Alperovitz's integrated system and the income flows within it:

1) Most basic industry and commercial land is owned at least in part by the community.

2) Federal power is devolved to smaller-scale regions (perhaps eight in the United States).

3) Large estates are essentially confiscated at death. This is related to the larger theme that no one person, or small class of people, should have the right to claim the bulk of what is in fact a common inheritance of wealth and knowledge generated by centuries of technological development. This mechanism is also seen as an important way to promote substantive equality among citizens, and thereby help strengthen the capacity of "each and all" to participate in a democratic process.

4) Income streams from community profits and inheritance add to social incomes for all, promoting not only security but also equality and real freedom (see Van Parijs).

5) Planning mechanisms exist at both the local and regional levels to stabilize communities.

6) Community-owned land and enterprise would also permit greater local-level democracy on such decisions as how communities are to be designed. This kind of decision making would promote experimentation with new models of community design aimed at promoting ecological goals and increased gender equity (ending the sharp geographical differentiation between the spheres of home, work, school, and market).

7) Once the system is fully functional, the reconstituted sense of community and reduced inequality may also (slowly) begin to generate a different culture (and sense of self-development) in which materialist striving is less important.

A central goal of this system is to develop the capacity for large scale, democratic social choice between alternative ways of life—for instance, between the rapidly growing, 40-hour work week, maximize production way of life, and the slowly growing, 25 hour work week-plus-more- participation-in-the-workplace way of life, or myriad other possibilities. In this model, given the structure of community ownership at the local level and the development of strong democratic norms in the system as a whole, it becomes possible for individual communities and regions to actively decide not to work as hard and sacrifice income for more free time (and less ecological damage), at the cost of reduced profits, by electing community managers who will implement such policies.

With this structure, Alperovitz is in a position to return to problem #2 enunciated above—how to overcome impulses towards continual growth in the system as a whole. Because the community has effective control of its own economic productive possibilities, it can decide what it wants to do in terms of organizing work, production level, setting norms for the work week, choosing to minimize pollution, aiming to maximize worker participation, etc. Obviously, larger planning mechanisms are needed to balance the decisions of each community, as well as to achieve regional and national environmental goals and carry out larger scale public investment and management of some larger public enterprises. But such decisions inevitably reflect the norms that develop in the communities themselves. If shorter work weeks and ecologically conscious production became the norm, the choices of the larger unit would likely reflect this over time, and vice versa.

To be sure, this model does not *guarantee* ecological sustainability. (Can any model?) That would depend on the communities and regions actually choosing the most ecologically friendly path of development (and hence require a culture of growing ecological awareness). What the model does attempt to do is alter the power relations such that legitimate social choices about the economy and its operations can be made democratically, and remove the common power obstacles to such social choices evident in both capitalist and state socialist societies. The "people" may or may not make the choices best reflecting ecological stewardship, but at least they would have an enhanced capacity to do so. Indeed, politics in this regime would largely consist of parties—Greens, Protestant Ethicists, etc.—organized around different conceptions of the good life.

As to strategy, Alperovitz sees the trajectory of the American political-economic system, characterized by increasing political disillusionment and growing loss of faith in the ability (and actual capacity) of the current system to solve important problems, as steadily pushing the country into a period of profound disorientation. Ultimately, a coherent vision and sense of direction—new ideas—must be generated if the stalemate is ever to be escaped. At the same time, growing economic pressure on states and localities has helped stimulate an impressive growth in community-oriented economic experimentation, including community land trusts, worker ownership, community development corporations (many of which directly own businesses), municipal enterprise, state equity holdings, state pension fund investments in local enterprises, and community supported agriculture, all of which show impressive growth just since the mid-1980s.

These experiments are likely to continue to develop, and if informed by a conscious understanding that they might become the building blocks of a structural solution to social, ecological, and economic decay, the experiments could provide the motor for a powerful new politics aimed at nurturing community-sustaining economic institutions, starting at the local and state levels. Simply put, the Alperovitz strategy largely de-emphasizes traditional models of trying to elect national-level progressives or do more organizing around issues. Instead, the strategy emphasizes a conscious effort to nurture grassroots-level alternative economic institutions that might be able to reconstruct, from the ground up, the experience of democratic participation and a community-level sense that "this is ours," as well as meet real community needs—and thereby open the door to a much more vigorous long-term politics aimed at slowly laying the building blocks of a coherent, alternative system.

Additional References

James O'Connor et al. *Is Capitalism Sustainable?* New York: Guilford Press, 1994. Essays from the magazine *Capitalism, Nature, and Socialism*; more critical than programmatic.

Barry Commoner. *Making Peace With the Planet.* New York: Pantheon Books, 1990. Strong statement of this noted ecologist's view of the inadequacy of existing environmental laws to rein in industry. Particularly interesting is Commoner's construction of a balance sheet for the chemical industry demonstrating that the industry would be making losses if it had to pay for the environmental costs it incurs on the public.

Jon Dryzek. *Rational Ecology.* New York: Basil Blackwell, 1987. Seminal discussion of how the existing designs of "social choice mechanisms" are not capable of effectively facing up to ecological crises.

David Gordon, ed. *Green Cities: Ecologically Sound Approaches to Urban Space.* Montreal: Black Rose Books, 1990.

Guy Dauncey. *After the Crash: The Emergence of the Rainbow Economy.* Basingstoke, Australia: Green Print, 1988. Points to small-scale, community-based economic alternatives as the route to ecological sustainability.

Mark Lucarelli. *Lewis Mumford and the Ecological Region.* New York: The Guilford Press, 1995. Discusses Mumford's ideas in their political context, shows why they failed, and describes their relevance for the ecological sustainability debate today.

Richard Douthwaite. *The Growth Illusion.* Devon: Resurgence, 1992. Sustained critique of the social and ecological consequences of economic growth by a British economist.

Kirkpatrick Sale. *Dwellers in the Land: The Bioregional Vision.* San Francisco: Sierra Club Books, 1985. Paradigmatic statement of the bioregional impulse in contemporary ecological activism.

Kirkpatrick Sale. *Human Scale.* New York: Coward, McGann and Georghegan, 1980. Impressive study drawing on sociological and anthropological sources of the appropriate scale of both polities in general and cities in particular; argues strongly the case for smaller cities.

John E Young. *The Next Efficiency Revolution:Creating a Sustainable Materials Economy.* Washington, DC: Worldwatch Institute, 1994.

Young's pamphlet is representative of a larger literature spelling out precisely the inefficient and unsustainable use of material inputs in the present economy.

Steve Lerner. *Eco-Pioneers.* Cambridge: MIT, 1997. Documents over a dozen technical innovations and initiatives which have resulted in more ecologically efficient forms of both industrial and agricultural production, as well as several local political initiatives in the United States. Good overview of concrete possibilities for near-term ecological improvement.

Paul Hawken. *The Ecology of Commerce: A Declaration of Sustainability.* New York, NY: HarperCollins Publishers, 1993. Develops principles by which businesses and corporations might learn to become good ecological stewards. Influential statement of the view that corporations can and should be reformed.

Bruno Fritsch. *Towards an Ecologically Sustainable Growth Society : Physical Foundations, Economic Transitions, and Political Constraints.* New York : Springer, 1994.

Clifford W. Cobb. *The Green National Product : A Proposed Index of Sustainable Economic Welfare.* Lanham, MD : University Press of America, 1994.

Update of the appendix to Daly and Cobb's *For the Common Good*; the ISEW corrects the GDP by considering ecological and social costs, with the finding that real sustainable welfare in the United States has been declining slightly over the past 30 years, even as the economy has grown.

Huey D. Johnson. *Green Plans : Greenprint for Sustainability.* Lincoln : University of Nebraska Press, 1995. Positive assessment of comprehensive environmental policy approaches now underway in the Netherlands, New Zealand, and Canada; urges American states and eventually the nation as a whole to follow suit.

Roy Morrison. *Ecological Democracy.* Boston: South End Press, 1995. Fine book outlining community-based participatory economics as an alternative to global neo-liberalism, with focus on Mondragon, the Seikatsu consumer cooperatives in Japan, and Coop Atlantic in Canada.

Brian Tokar. *The Green Alternative: Creating an Ecological Future.* San Pedro: R.E. Miles & Co., 1987. Tokar, a green journalist who writes for *Z* magazine and other periodicals, here spells out the core views of American Green Party activists.

Brian Doherty and Marius de Geus, eds. *Democracy and Green Political Thought*. London: Routledge, 1996. Superb edited volume of British thinkers assessing the relationship between ecological requirements and democratic theory. Contains particularly strong essays by Neil Carter on "Worker Cooperatives and Green Political Theory" and by de Geus contrasting "Ecological Restructuring of the State" with social change approaches based on "piecemeal engineering" or "radical utopianism."

James Robertson. *Future Wealth*. London: Cassell, 1990. Influential text describing possibilities for an ecologically sustainable economy.

Trent Schroyer, ed. *A World That Works*. New York: Bootstrap Press, 1997. Reader from the 1997 Denver gathering of The Other Economic Summit.

Dennis Pirages, ed. *Building Sustainable Societies: A Blueprint for a Post-Industrial World*. Armonk, NY: M.E. Sharpe, 1996. Edited volume includes essays from Ophuls, Alperovitz, Daly, Milbrath, and numerous other American thinkers discussing "the question of whether the industrial model of human progress can be sustained over time."

Jerry Mander and Edward Goldsmith, eds. *Against the Global Economy*. San Francisco: Sierra Club Books, 1996. Edited volume providing critiques of globalization and discussion of grassroots alternatives from leading activists.

Peter Calthorpe. *The Next American Metropolis: Ecology, Community, and the American Dream*. New York: Princeton Architectural Press, 1993. Fine introduction to green community design and architecture, within a capitalist context, from a leading practitioner.

Sim Van der Ryn and Stuart Cowan. *Ecological Design*. Washington: Island Press, 1996.

Curtis Moore and Alan Miller. *Green Gold: Japan, Germany, the United States, and the Race for Environmental Technology*. Boston: Beacon Press, 1994. Describes how strong environmental regulation can stimulate business to develop environmental technologies faster, with important economic benefits for the nation that can get ahead in this area fastest; currently United States trails badly in the race. Harsh critique of American environmental policy from this perspective.

John Buell and Tom Deluca. *Sustainable Democracy*. Thousand Oaks, CA: Sage, 1996. Ten-principle plan for spelling out an environmental ethic capable of generating wide support in a capitalist democracy; very much within social democratic tradition.

Chapter Four

Utopian Literature

Introduction and Overview

Literary depictions of a "utopian" society have a long lineage, dating back to Thomas More's 16th-century novel which coined the very word, "Utopia." In the 20th century, to the genre of utopian literature have been added the notions of "dystopia," "heterotopia," and, in Ursula LeGuin's usage, "the ambiguous utopia." The category "dystopia" is most obviously associated with the work of Orwell (*Animal Farm*, *1984*) and Huxley (*Brave New World*), but also has thrived over the past 25 years in a variety of feminist and science fiction works. The latter two concepts, heterotopia and the "ambiguous utopia," also hallmarks of recent feminist and science fiction writing, are intended to connote an appropriate distance from the idea, now typically seen as dangerous if not totalitarian, that one can naively paint a picture of the perfect society or historical era.

Despite these complications, a clearly recognizable "utopian" literature—fiction offering concrete portrayals of a more ideal (though not necessarily flawless) society—has flourished in the past quarter century, particularly in the work of feminist authors writing in the genre (loosely) of science fiction. The literature, in fact, is vast, and its growth has been accompanied as well in the last decade by the emergence of an impressive secondary literature subjecting recent utopian novels to scholarly analysis.

Relying in part on the judgments of this secondary literature, this bibliography highlights representative works from Ursula K. LeGuin, Ernest Callenbach, Joanna Russ, Samuel Delany, Margaret Atwood, Marge Piercy, W.Warren Wagar, and Kim Stanley Robinson. LeGuin's *The Dispossessed* and Callenbach's *Ecotopia* share the literary device of narrating from the point of view of travelers from related but radically different societies. In LeGuin's case, the traveler goes from an anarchistic, fully cooperative world to a hyper-capitalist mother planet; in Callenbach's case, the trip is in the opposite direction, from a resource-wasting continental United States to the ecologically sustainable Pacific Northwest region dubbed "Ecotopia." Russ and Piercy use the device of characters who communicate through time to explore different possible futures and to depict both the "bad" and the "good" societies. Atwood's *The Handmaid's Tale*, on the other hand, proceeds as a stark dystopia; Delany's *Triton* consciously plays off LeGuin to introduce the notion of "heterotopia," an acknowledgment that *multiple*, not unitary visions (seen by Delany and others as necessarily stifling), are appropriate for imagining what "utopia" might look like. Wagar's *A Short History of the Future*, while a less rich account of how the future might look in actual human experience, is an interesting, "history written as fiction" discussion of the possible course of world politics over the next two centuries. Robinson has produced two sets of trilogies discussing the nature of the good society, one focusing on an envisaged colonization of Mars, the other on what California might or might not look like in the mid-21st century.

The annotations below focus rather tightly on the actual visions of both the "good" and "bad" society painted by each author, with little focus on the works as literature per se. (As indicated, there is considerable academic literary analysis of the genre; see the list of additional references at the end of this chapter.) Special attention is given to concrete descriptions of political and economic institutions, and to notions offered (if any) of how such a better (or at least different) society would come about.

Ernest Callenbach. *Ecotopia*. Berkeley: Banyon Books, 1975.

Callenbach's 1975 novel sketches a future in which the Pacific Northwest has seceded from the rest of the United States and established a society based on principles of conservation, production for use, and a retreat from materialism. Citizens of Ecotopia work less, play more, have looser norms regarding love and family, and waste far less than their U.S. contemporaries. All industry has, with state direction, been redesigned to maximally reduce ecological impact. For instance, transportation in Ecotopia consists of an elaborate train system for mass passenger rail, complemented by a system of individualized rail cars for intracity travel, with the motor vehicle all but abandoned. Capitalist impulses towards growth have been removed as the society provides guaranteed economic security for all, and more than this, a richer sense of community and human purpose, aided greatly by radically expanded free time (20 hour work weeks). Firms are worker-owned (with employees treated as "partners"); the accumulation of large sums of wealth across generations has been curbed by the abolition of inheritance.

The political system in Ecotopia is largely female-dominated, resulting in part from the role the women-led "Survivalist Party" played in bringing about the transition to Ecotopia. This fact is indicative of a broader sea change in the social values of Ecotopia: the stress is now on cooperation and respect for nature. The Ecotopians adapt an attitude towards nature and land not unlike that of Native Americans—the fact that trees, for instance, are alive is taken very seriously: trees are on occasion referred to by citizens as "brother." The basic ideology guiding Ecotopia is that "humans were meant to take their modest place in a seamless, stable-state web of living organisms, disturbing that web as little as possible... People were to be happy not to the extent they dominated their fellow creatures on the earth, but to the extent they lived in balance with them." [78] The narrator, journalist William Weston from New York City, USA, notes that "[It is no] surprise that to such a morality most industrial processes, work schedules, and products are suspect! Who would use an earth-mover on his own mother?" [79]

The story consists, rather neatly, of Weston's personal experiences and interactions with Ecotopians, interspersed with his reports back home on what he finds in Ecotopia 19 years (1999) after the secession of the Northwest (said to take place in 1980). (The remaining United States, in a state of muted bitterness over the Northwest's secession, knows little beyond negative propaganda about what goes on in Ecotopia.)

Callenbach's straightforward portrayal of a society unambiguously good and eminently achievable is as close to a "naive" utopia as one is likely to find in recent literature. Probably the most unrealistic aspect of the novel is the depth and totality of the vast cultural change said to take place in a period of two decades, and the near-universal, consensual support for these new values. Where have all the beef-eating, football-watching, power-boat driving people gone? To be sure, Callenbach portrays the new culture as having earned its spurs on the crucible of the struggle for Independence, and a period of heightened crisis followed by revolution and then two decades of uninterrupted development might, in fact, lead to vast cultural changes in less than a generation, if not quite to the degree Callenbach imagines.

However, the obvious must be noted: as time passes and actual historical reality—the rise of yuppie-ism, the 1980s' swing back to materialist values, etc.—diverges farther and farther from Callenbach's scenario, that scenario seems less and less plausible. (Callenbach wrote a sequel story in 1981 focusing specifically on the struggle to create Ecotopia, *Ecotopia Emerging*; a growing contradiction between a deepening ecological crisis and increasing numbers of ecologically aware, alternative value-embracing citizens eventually unleashes the political explosion making Independence possible).

Yet the specific green technologies (which Callenbach clearly delights in discussing in some detail), the reduced working hours, and even much of the new ethic Callenbach portrays are all quite achievable and realistic in a technical sense; the roadblock to their implementation is their lack of political viability. Callenbach's conception of a region breaking away from within the United States is a notable "strategic" vision, with the implicit messages that first, a strong sense of "place" and attention to a community's immediate ecology must be part of any serious movement towards sustainability, and, second, that the United States as a whole is probably too committed to its current path to make the move all at once. More troubling, however, (and perhaps less plausible) is Callenbach's portrayal of a near-rigid separation between the breakaway society (Ecotopia) and the mother country (capitalist USA) as an enabling condition for Ecotopia's development. Indeed, some critics (including David Pepper) have seen a "lifeboat ethic" at work in the novel, as well as elements of an "eco-fascist" mentality in the portrayal of a largely homogeneous, single-party dominated culture tied together by semi-tribal rituals and a sense of mystical connection to the land.

Ursula K. LeGuin. *The Dispossessed: An Ambiguous Utopia*. New York: Harper & Row, 1974.

LeGuin's novel utilizes a single narrator describing events on two sister worlds, Urras, a hyper-capitalist world with the familiar flaws of American society in exaggerated form, and Annares, a moon colonized decades previously by a breakaway Urrasti group. Annares is a participatory, anarchist society, in which children are socialized to think of community first and to reject egoism. Living in a resource-scarce world, Annares citizens are content simply to meet their basic needs, with additional income generated from the shipment of minerals back to Urras (the only remaining contact between the two societies).

The Annarres economy consists of worker-controlled, decentralized units producing fish, minerals, crafts, and agriculture, working five to seven hour days (and more when needed), with one of every ten days given over to communal work (such as garbage collection). The various decentralized units are coordinated by a central planning agency. This agency has representatives from organized syndicates (with their own organizations for identifying local needs and inducing democratic participation) in each community; the ideal is for ideas and wishes to move from each community up to the center and thereby hold the central agency accountable. Labor mobility is permitted, but workers' desires for placements are balanced and processed by a central computer. The society is governed without money, and there are few personal possessions; most household functions are communalized (via community kitchens and dormitory-style housing).

The society is nonsexist to the point of assigning children gender-neutral names, and the institution of marriage does not exist, although some Annaresti form bonded partnerships. Most children above age two are raised in a collective, dormitory setting. Law enforcement institutions are kept to a minimum—the guiding disciplinary mechanism is the collective social conscience. (And, freed of various oppressions and material needs, the motives for crime generally do not arise.)

LeGuin makes clear that what makes this system work, when it does, is a changed human ethic and spirit—namely, supreme emphasis on principles of reciprocity and mutual aid. "...with the myth of the State out of the way, the real mutuality and reciprocity of society become clear. Sacrifice may be demanded of the individual, but never compromise: for though only the society could give security and stability, only the individual, the person, has the power of moral choice—the power of change, an essential function of life. The Odonian society was conceived as a permanent revolution, and revolution begins in the thinking mind." [80]

The extent to which this actually comes about is the substance of Annarres's ambiguity as a utopia: As time passes, the unmistakable tendency in this strongly communal society is for groupthink—the intellectual corollary of bureaucratism—to rise at the expense of the free-thinking, nonconformist individuals that form the base of true mutual aid and anarchist freedom. Shevek, the narrator, becomes acutely aware of this tendency over the course of the book, primarily through his struggles in the academic politics of Annarresti physics to overcome a colleague's personal fiefdom. At the same time, real bureaucratization is setting in in the Annarresti capital among career members of the central ministries. The plot alternates between Shevek's descriptions of his past life on Annarres and his reporting of contemporary events from his historic journey to the mother country, Urras. The trip is motivated by the prospects of scientific exchange among physicists working on a breakthrough theory that the Urras hope may help them achieve light-speed travel (and advantage in an ongoing war with another planet).

Shevek experiences some of the pleasures and vitality of Urrasti society, but his primary experience as the trip proceeds is of the mother world's naked brutality, manifested by the close surveillance under which he is kept, the desire of the Urrasti physicists to rip his work off, and an Urrasti air bombing of resistance groups which Shevek witnesses. Allowed at the end to return home (after a distinctly fairy tale ending when Shevek succeeds in completing the "General Temporal Theory" and shares the practical result, the "ansible," with both the Urrasti and their war opponents), Shevek reenters Annarres intent on redoubling efforts at his "Syndicate of Initiative" to combat the ossification and bureaucratization of Annarresti thought, culture, and society.

LeGuin's envisioned utopia clearly echoes major strands of green-anarchist thinking in the United States, particularly the "libertarian municipalism" of Bookchin. What is notable here is an acceptance of the need for central state-like institutions, but with an awareness that such institutions need to be continually checked by fresh rebellions (a notion not unlike Jefferson's hope for revolutions each generation). Further, the tension LeGuin illustrates between the desirability of strong community norms and a changed human nature and the danger of growing a culture that cannot tolerate nonconformists and innovators is an obvious concern for any communitarian vision of the good society.

Also implicit in LeGuin's scenario is the notion that while a communitarian anarchist society is possible in theory, there is no way to get from "here to there" from within contemporary capitalist (Urrasti) society. A fresh breaking off, root and branch, from the old to the new, as in a colonization-type scenario, is required. Moreover, the libertarian-communal anarchism she espouses is obviously incompatible with a mass production/consumer society—that too must be given up, not just the governing institutions (property, marriage, prisons, the state) of industrial capitalism.

Joanna Russ. *The Female Man*. New York: Bantam Books, 1975. (Manuscript completed in 1971.)

Russ's narrative uses four female characters situated at different points in time to describe the struggle to create and sustain a feminist utopia. Jeanine lives in a 1969 in which the second world war never came and gender norms are still hyper-traditional; the chief narrator, Joanne, lives in the actually existing version of 1969 America; Jael lives in an in-between period when women and men are locked in a bloody civil war; and Janet lives far in the future in the accomplished feminist utopia. The multiplicity of narrative voices is used as both a device for communicating a broad sweep of historical progress, from the present to utopia, and as an expression of the possibilities open to women's experience—passivity in response to oppression in the case of Jeanine, a warrior spirit in the case of Jael, sublime self-confidence in the case of Janet...The key obviously becomes, what will Joanne (and all of us) decide to be like?

The utopia of "Whileaway" in which Janet lives is an all-female society, made possible by the development of parthenogenesis, a process in which two eggs united create a child. Where did all the men go? Contrary to the later benign myth of eradication by plague, they were in fact destroyed in armed struggle by Jael's generation.

The operation of Whileaway depends heavily on technology; the "induction helmet" makes heavy physical labor easy by linking machinery to the human brain wave. This work is performed by younger women; as women age they move more and more into creative and intellectual pursuits in a variety of jobs (including the job of planning the economy), which takes no more than 16 hours a week. Production aims to achieve a balance between industrial and agricultural sectors; there is no urbanization as we know it in Whileaway. It is a neo-pastoral vision; the economy is not understood as an abstraction but simply as enabler to the larger goals of an ecologically sensitive, pleasure-maximizing, play-oriented society in which everyone enjoys a rich and varied life experience. Government is minimalist—as in LeGuin's Annarres, social norms enforce healthy behavior within the community with little need of formal punishment, etc. Social life is organized through large kinship groups which surround parenting couples.

In Whileaway, Janet tells us, everyone grows up strong, free, creative, with spark and initiative, capable in a wide range of labor, artistic, and intellectual activities. Full blown rites of passage mark changes in life; substantial creative freedom is given to adolescents (including sex), before formal entry into the work force at age 17. Human development reaches its peak potential—Whileaway women have extraordinarily high IQs and well-formed bodies. The resulting culture is marked by a luxurious *joie de vivre* and maximal human freedom (even freedom to kill!).

The interplay among the four narratives highlights the political commitment needed to bring the world of Whileaway about. Jael, of the hell-like warrior era, needs to draw upon the help of the other three in order to continue the fight, calling for an extension of the war into all time zones... to the substantial discomfort of both Janet and 1969-living Joanne. (The more oppressed Jeanine, on the other hand, has no problem with this.) The message is clear: conflict, and when appropriate violent conflict, must be embraced to readjust the power relations such that women can be liberated. The first step in entering the struggle is an awareness of all aspects of women's situation: on one side the vision of liberation, on another side the face of brutal oppression, on another the spirit of engaged struggle, and finally, the side of those who must make choices on how to live and struggle (or not) in the contradiction-filled in-between period (the present).

Marge Piercy. *Women on the Edge of Time*. New York: Knopf, 1976.

Piercy's novel also uses the device of women from different time periods communicating with each other to illuminate the contrast between the oppressions of contemporary society and the possibilities of a different future. The narrator of the "present," Connie, is a poor Hispanic woman caught in a no-win battle with state bureaucracies (she is unjustly institutionalized in a mental hospital). Connie's life changes when, within the hospital, she opens up a telepathic channel of communication with Luciente and is able to visit her in the future village of Mattapoisett, some 150 years into the future.

Mattapoisett is a neo-peasant village, part of a larger system of decentralized, ecologically balanced villages organized on communalist principles and utilizing high technology in an appropriate manner. Each region in the society is maximally self-sufficient economically; the economy is not monetized and each and all are guaranteed necessities. There is no conception of growing the economy to acquire luxuries. Instead, there is plenty of time left over to play, as work has been reduced to as little as 1-5 hours a week per citizen. Larger scale government exists but is scarce—its main task is to oversee a process whereby the various needs of each village is balanced with the available resources and that consensual decisions about resource allocation are made (a notion similar to the "participatory planning" economic visions of both Michael Albert and Robin Hahnel and British economist Pat Devine). Government leaders are chosen by lot.

Gender relationships are radically revamped: not only is the institution of marriage done away with in favor of freely chosen relationships of various degrees of length and seriousness; the conception of children is completely separated from romantic relationships. Children are conceived in an incubator when three friends choose to have a child; these (unromantically attached) friends act as "comothers" until the children reach age 13, at which point they undergo initiation into the society as full adults, and parental bonds are dissolved. (Children are not permitted to speak to their former parents for three months after initiation.) The abdication of a unique capacity to give birth is seen as the decisive move in obliterating gender hierarchies. "...[A]s long as were biologically enchained, we'd never be equal," Connie is informed. "And males would never be humanized to be loving and tender." [81]

Indeed, men are able to use artificial breasts to nurse children. Similarly, racial categories have effectively disappeared after a long period of deliberate genetic mixing. As Jennifer Burwell points out, the discomfort Connie experiences in encountering this elimination of gender and race categories illustrates the tension between future visions of a society in which "difference" has become literally unimportant, and the felt necessity, in the present, for marginalized persons to construct personal and political identities that draw heavily on their own particularities. (Connie draws strength from identifying herself as a Hispanic woman, for instance).

The society of Mattapoisett is in the finishing stages of a 30-year war against the forces of the old order. And like in *The Female Man*, the actual attainment of the utopia, from the standpoint of Connie is uncertain—there is also a dystopian, corporate-dominated possible future which Piercy briefly describes. (Piercy, not surprisingly, has a classically New Left, Marxian-oriented view of capitalism.) Connie (like all of us) needs to decide whether to struggle to help make the ideal future possible. Invigorated by her insight into a possible future, Connie returns to the present reality of her mental hospital determined to resist her oppressors, killing with poison the members of the medical team "caring" for her (via involuntary brain implants designed to control behavior). The consequence for Connie is a lifetime of institutionalization as a periodically violent prisoner, but we are told that this act of resistance has created ripples of change that percolate into the distant reaches of the continuum of time—and thus help make the possibility of a Mattapoisett a reality.

Samuel Delany. *Triton*. New York: Bantam, 1976.

Delany's "heterotopia" of Triton is set on a distant moon of Neptune; Triton is one of three dozen colonies in the outer planets engaged in a war for independence from the dying inner worlds of Earth and Mars. Described, uniquely, through the lens of an unhappy resident, Bron, Triton features an egalitarian society with extreme libertarian impulses. Production is carried out almost entirely by cybernetic units; economic units themselves are socially owned, with a few "private cooperatives" permitted in some sectors. Minimum incomes are guaranteed whether one works or not; persons who do not work (20 hour weeks) can claim income at the state's expense. Instead of a market, there is a vast computer system which keeps track of each citizen's work credits and consumption credits; no money transactions between persons are required. Roughly one-fifth of the population at any time is on "welfare," and virtually all Triton residents are on it at some point in their lives...there is no stigma attached.

Triton stresses freedom of personal lifestyle, especially regarding clothing, family structure (marriage and prostitution are forbidden, but self-chosen family units do exist) and sexual practices (anything goes, including frequent sex change operations). Indeed, the essence of the culture in Triton is that established social and cultural norms, other than tolerance, are not much in evidence; the dichotomy between norm and deviance has been substantially broken down.

Triton is a heterotopia, then, precisely because it is not guided by an overarching vision of the good life, but rather gives supreme value to individual freedom. As a story, then, *Triton* is not so much about social institutions abstracted, but about what life might be like for ordinary *individuals*, given a set of institutions substantially better than our own. While many remarkable individuals are met along the way, the presence of the misfit Bron (characterized as a male chauvinist, dominance-oriented person unable to overcome his Earth-based socialization) indicates that utopia is no guarantee of happiness for all. As Tom Moylan neatly summarizes, "The social macrostructure [of Triton] radically guarantees freedom with all the inherent trust and risks it places on the individual. However, the macrostructure does not directly determine how the personal microstructures of each life will work out." [82]

Not only are some not able to thrive in a climate of "emancipation," the unpleasant fact of the war with the inner planets (causing the deaths of 90% of Earth's population) lingers in the background (the fighting is done by weaponry, not soldiers). More to the point, in a society that maximizes individuality, the levers of social change are unclear: if all sorts of deviance can be tolerated and absorbed by the culture easily, it becomes extremely difficult to change that culture. Perhaps this is not a problem given the relatively just institutions of Triton, but as Keith Booker points out, the parallel between this situation and that of present-day American culture is striking.[83]

It is an interesting question as to whether a society might exist that could both have a relatively communalistic economy and maximize personal freedom to the nth degree; while such a combination seems strange, in a society where the economy was only a small part of life, perhaps the dichotomy would be plausible. Even if possible, Delany's thought experiment in creating Triton raises questions as to its desirability. Is the abdication of communal norms in the culture really a good thing? But the larger point of Delany's work is not this specific question, but simply that in any set of institutions, no matter how well certain values are maximized, trade-offs will have to be made, one set of goods exchanged for another, with the consequence that not everyone will be happy, and that no uniquely ideal balance of institutions and values is possible—even if definite improvements can be made.

Margaret Atwood. *The Handmaid's Tale*. New York: Houghton Mifflin, 1985.

Atwood's book in fact is not utopian at all, but one of the most influential examples of the large dystopian "impulse" in contemporary literature. The graphic picture Atwood draws is set concretely in the territorial United States of the not too distant future, where formal American democracy has given way to a new theocracy. In Atwood's vision of the "Republic of Gilead," vast ecological destruction, toxic poisoning, and various diseases have created a situation where only a tiny percentage of women can bear children. This threat to the national future leads to totalitarian control over the lives of fertile women convicted of petty crimes (including fornication and adultery as well as political dissent). These women serve as "handmaids" to elite males in Gilead with sterile wives. Handmaids are concubines forced to submit to a humiliating "ceremony" in which men have clinical-style sex with the fertile women, in an attempt to conceive a child. When a child is in fact born, it is handed over to the father and the sterile wife and treated as their child, and the handmaid is returned to another "assignment."

This rather horrific practice is located within the context of a neo-fascist regime organized on white supremacist, patriarchal, homophobic, and theocentric principles; the government is carrying out the forced resettlement of blacks and repatriation of Jews, maintaining toxic dump "colonies" to which criminals and political prisoners are sent, and, in the name of God, waging a vicious civil war against rebellious elements. At the same time, the regime has constructed an elaborate ideology sanctifying and protecting the miracle of birth; elite women are given substantial power and play a critical role in enforcing this ideology, as it is they who organize and enforce the handmaid system. Abortion, obviously, is condemned, and there is no doubt that it is men who run the society. Pictures are substituted for words in public places to prevent non-elite women from the crime of reading. But as Atwood puts it in the postscript, "Historical Notes on the Handmaid's Tale," "Gilead was, although undoubtedly patriarchal in form, occasionally matriarchal in content. ... As the architects of Gilead knew, to institute an effective totalitarian system or indeed any system at all you must offer some benefits and freedoms, at least to a privileged few, in return for those you remove." [84]

The story turns upon one handmaid, captured trying to escape Gilead, who is assigned to the security Commander, suffers through the humiliation of the "ceremony" before conceiving a child illicitly via another man (with the support of the Commander's wife), and eventually escapes (or so she hopes) to join the active armed resistance.

Over ten years after publication of this novel, it is easy to see Atwood's story as reflecting the nightmares of a North American leftist looking at the political emergence of the religious right (and concomitant efforts to control women's bodies) of the 1980s, with ecological destruction and apartheid-style racial policies added into the mix. This is what could happen if the Falwells and Helmses ever took control, Atwood seems to be saying.

But on a deeper level, the value of the book is not simply showing what might happen if the far-right took control, but in relating the circumstances of such a shift to concrete, legitimate crises which our current path is quite capable of creating—in this case, the specter of sterility. If Atwood's fictional picture is extreme, the notion that pockets of fascist politics might emerge in the United States in response to any number of crises during the next century is not. Further, as the "Historical Notes" makes clear, Atwood indicates that a fascist society cannot last forever; by the year 2195 historians see Gilead as a fascinating period of an increasingly distant past. (Indeed, Atwood takes a subtle dig at academic culture in her depiction of historians who are able to distance themselves from the reality of the handmaid's suffering to a disturbing degree.) In other words, even fascism is not the end of the story—but it's nasty while it lasts.

W. Warren Wagar. *A Short History of the Future.* Chicago: University of Chicago Press, 1989. (Updated and revised version, 1993.)

Wagar's book is half novel, half social forecasting. Broadly speaking, Wagar (writing near the end of the Cold War), imagines the continuation of the Cold War structure, with corporate capital becoming increasingly dominant worldwide until the year 2044, when a nuclear world war III breaks out. In the aftermath, a strong global socialist movement rises to set up world federalist institutions and to correct basic inequalities, finally gaining power in the 2060s. This "commonwealth" lasts for some 70 years before the "Small" movement arises, calling for a return of power to decentralized communities and a rollback of the world government's power. By the year 2150, "Autonomy Laws vest all government authority in chartered local communities." A system of decentralized, egalitarian communities thus becomes the highest form of human civilization.

As Immanuel Wallerstein has pointed out regarding this text, it is a searching exploration not only of global capitalism but also of the two main varieties of proposed alternatives: centralized state socialism or social democracy, and grassroots-oriented decentralist models of community. Of particular interest is Wagar's judgment that it is necessary to pass through the former stage to get to the latter; in other words, first generate sufficient use of state power to challenge corporate rule and correct existing injustices, then pass through to the good society of small communities.

Compared with the other novels discussed here, Wagar's is valuable for being self-consciously rooted in the foreseeable future and emphasizing the politics and "history" of the next two centuries. It is less strong in developing characters as a means to illustrate what living in that future history would feel like in actual experience.

Kim Stanley Robinson. *Pacific Edge*. New York: Tom Doherty and Associates, 1990.

Robinson's "Three Californias" trilogy offers a view of what California might look like in the mid-21st century after a nuclear holocaust; what it might look like if present trends continue; and, in *Pacific Edge*, an engaging look at the on-the-ground quality of life and local politics of a single community, within a California that has made drastic shifts towards an ecologically balanced way of life. While specific models vary from town to town, the community of El Modena, the focus of this book, owns its own utilities and land; collects a stiff, progressive tax on all businesses; requires all citizens to work 10 hours a week at a public job; and pays out an annual dividend to all based on revenues from utilities, land, and taxation. There is a maximum income for all citizens, as well as restrictions on the size of firms. Work is slow-paced, and (due to the guaranteed dividend) undertaken of one's own volition. Key decisions take place in town council meetings open to the public.

Robinson goes beyond a static portrait of a local-level model to show how the dynamics of politics in such a society would work, as well as how the local level units must interact with other local and regional units, particularly given the fundamental reality of scarce water that must be shared among many communities. There is a multiplicity of political parties in El Modena, not all of whom are committed to ecological balance as the top priority. (The "New Federalists" are oriented towards increasing the size of the town dividend by promoting more development.) The conflict between the green and pro-growth factions in El Modena forms the dramatic background for the book; yet Robinson is at his best in describing the everyday life and personalities of El Modena's citizens. In the end, Robinson shows that the good society will not bring an end to greed, tragedy, or heartbreak, and that any modern society can only be ecologically sustainable on a contingent basis. But this novel also tries to show that a good society should be able to produce many rich experiences of connection with nature and with other people, as well as people with sufficient creativity and sense of freedom to respond to the ongoing challenges of life—both everyday and political—with some success.

Additional References

Joanna Russ. *To Write Like a Woman: Essays in Feminism and Science Fiction*. Bloomington: Indiana University Press, 1995.

Suzy McKee Charnas. *Motherlines*. New York: Berkeley, 1979.

Sally Miller Gearhart. *The Wanderground: Stories of the Hill Women*. Watertown, MA: Persephone Press, 1979.

Octavia Butler. *Kindred*. Boston: Beacon Press, 1979.

Tom Moylan. *Demand the Impossible: Science Fiction and the Utopian Imagination*. New York: Metheun, 1986.

M. Keith Booker. *The Dystopian Impulse in Modern Literature: Fiction as Social Criticism*. Westport, CT: Greenwood Press, 1994.

Thomas Pynchon. *Vineland*. Boston: Little, Brown, 1990. Dystopian novel portraying a semi-fascist U.S. governed largely by the populace's addiction to television and popular culture.

Angelika Bammer. *Partial Visions: Feminism and Utopianism in the 1970s*. New York: Routledge, 1991.

Jane Donawerthe and Carol A. Kolmerten, eds. *Utopian and Science Fiction by Women*. Syracuse: Syracuse University Press, 1994.

Elizabeth McCutcheon. "More's Utopia, Callenbach's Ecotopia, and Biosphere 2" in A.D. Cousins and Damian Grace, eds. *More's Utopia and the Utopian Inheritance*. Lanham, MD: University Press of America, 1995.

R. Frye. "The Economics of Ecotopia." *Alternative Futures*, Vol. 3 (1980), pp.71-81.

Margaret Keulen, *Radical Imagination : Feminist Conceptions of the Future in Ursula Le Guin, Marge Piercy, and Sally Miller Gearhart*. New York : P. Lang, 1991.

Frances Bartkowski. *Feminist Utopias*. Lincoln: University of Nebraska Press, 1989.

Jennifer Burwell. *Notes on Nowhere : Feminism, Utopian Logic, and Social Transformation*. Minneapolis: University of Minnesota Press, 1997.

J. Brooks Bouson. *Brutal Choreographies: Oppositional Strategies and Narrative Design in the Novels of Margaret Atwood*. Amherst: University of Massachusetts Press, 1993.

Daniel Quinn. *Ishmael*. New York: Bantam, 1992.

Chapter Five

Additional Visions

Introduction and Overview

The final chapter of this bibliography is a "catch-all" collection of "visionary" social science literature from a variety of disciplines, with annotations on fifteen representative works. The first two, Alfred Andersen's *Liberating the Early American Dream* and J.W. Smith's *The World's Wasted Wealth* are exemplary instances of the burgeoning range of utopian visions produced (and often self-published) by writers outside academia. Obviously, the genre of self-published plans for a better world includes much that is frivolous and not worthy of comment, but these two writers, among others, have produced thoughtful, insightful critiques and proposals that merit serious consideration.

Also included in this initial section is German academic and activist Margrit Kennedy's novel idea for "inflation-free money"—money which, like other goods, is designed to slowly lose value over time, eliminating the rentier power money holders now maintain in modern economies. Finally, newsletter publisher and long-time Washington, DC activist Sam Smith presents an array of strategies for "taking back" American democracy.

The next part of this chapter includes annotations to several recent contributions from academic social and political philosophers. Political theorist Iris Marion Young's *Justice and the Politics of Difference* critiques both liberal theories of justice and communitarianism from the standpoint of concern for acknowledging social diversity; what is most interesting about the book, however, is the way Young's prescription for the polity melds postmodern and feminist concerns with close attention to the power relations of capitalist political economy. Political theorists Joshua Cohen and Joel Rogers' *Associations and Democracy* deeply explores the notion of how citizens can be adequately represented politically in *any* regime purporting to be democratic, taking as their starting point the notion that the *organization* of citizens to defend their own interests is a fundamental prerequisite of any alternative political-economic regime (or move to such).

143

French scholar Phillipe Van Parijs' *Real Freedom for All* brilliantly elaborates and defends the concept of an unconditional guaranteed income as the basis for guaranteeing the practical freedom of individuals in advanced economies. Next, University of North Carolina philosopher E.M. (Maynard) Adams' 1997 book *A Society Fit for Human Beings* comprehensively critiques each sector of contemporary American culture and its institutions, unblinkingly calling for a radically different economic system, combined with a revived ethic of communitarian-humanism. Adams' position can be summarized as doses of market socialism, William Bennett, and the anti-consumerist *Adbusters* magazine, all rolled into one.

In sharp contrast to this lofty vision is the severely pessimistic position taken by University of Oregon political scientist John Dryzek, who spells out the "null option" for a progressive future. In Dryzek's view, capitalism, however undesirable, cannot be transcended, and only democratically inspired resistance to the state is a plausible political strategy in the foreseeable future. Putting pessimism aside, Duke University professors Thomas Naylor and William Willimon provocatively urge a "downsizing" of America's major social and political institutions. Finally, feminist political theorist Nancy Fraser develops a vision of a genuinely egalitarian postindustrial "welfare state" in which both men and women participate in work and caregiving activities.

The next four works included in this chapter are attempts to analyze systems from a theological/ethical point of view, including one Jewish thinker and three representatives of modern social Christianity. Rabbi Michael Lerner, editor of *Tikkun* magazine, is probably the most prominent American intellectual discussing public affairs from an explicit ethical and religious view in the 1990s. Although Lerner stakes out an "agnostic" position on the question of capitalism, his chief political goal is to "change the bottom line" of American society—including its economic practices—to incorporate criteria of caring and spiritual sensitivity into everyday institutional practices.

The body of Gary Dorrien's work, capped most recently by his 1995 book *Soul in Society*, includes impressive reviews of American democratic socialist thought, Anglo-American religious socialism in the 20th century, neo-conservatism in the postwar era, and various strains of radical thought in 20th century Protestant thought, with particular attention paid to the various forms of liberation theology that have arisen in the past generation. Dorrien is explicitly searching for a political and economic form that radical "social gospel" Christians can in good faith advocate at century's end, and if Dorrien's destination is perhaps not quite the promised land, his journey is still well worth observing. Canadian theologian Harold Wells has similar concerns in his *A Future for Socialism? Political Theology and the Triumph of Capitalism*, published in 1996. Although Wells is much more wedded to the term "socialism" than Dorrien, his book complements Dorrien's work well by skillfully analyzing the variety of actually existing and proposed versions of "socialism" from the point of view of Christian faith. Even more impressive is German activist Ulrich Duchrow's *Alternatives to Global Capitalism*, a work demonstrating equal facility with Old Testament concepts of economy and social justice and the contemporary literature on feasible alternatives to capitalism.

Alfred Andersen. *Liberating the Early American Dream*, Ukiah, CA: Thomas Paine Institute, 1985. Second edition, 1989.

Andersen's book critiques contemporary capitalist economics and offers an alternative proposal that explicitly takes account of the extent to which we, as a community, inherit wealth and resources from the past. The centerpiece of Andersen's vision is community ownership of land, with rents paid into two separate trust funds: a local trust fund and a global trust fund. Each individual would then receive an annual payment from each fund as a second income. Such a dual system would recognize the claim of specific communities to recover the wealth they themselves produce (adjusting for different costs of living) *and* the fact that larger communities (nation, globe) also have a right to share in the wealth of very rich communities. Thus Andersen's proposal undercuts national and global inequalities by guaranteeing each and all a substantial stake in the "unearned increment" of land rents.

Andersen calculates that initially each American family of four on would receive on average $14,000 (1985) dollars annually just from local funds and their (proportionately less) share of the proposed global fund. Andersen also details at some length the rules by which the system would work; for instance, full shares in a community trust fund might go only to natural-born residents or local residents with a given number of years living in that community. Newcomers would be entitled to only a partial share (as well as a partial share of the fund from the community which they left). This would help prevent migration from one community to another in search of higher dividend checks. Assuming that land values continue to rise at the historical rate of 11-15% a year, the postinflation real increase in the land dividend should be 6-10% annually, according to Andersen.

Andersen's proposal, which he ties to the revival of traditional American political values such as liberty and equality, is relatively simple, probably quite workable, and consistent with a number of other visions forwarded by market socialists and others (such as Leland Stauber and Gar Alperovitz). It also is amenable to any number of technical modifications: national level trust funds, for instance, might serve as an intermediate stage before the development of global trust funds. The main impediment, as usual, is the political power of those vested interests standing to lose from this proposal.

J.W. Smith. *The World's Wasted Wealth 2*. Cambria, CA: Institute for Economic Democracy, 1994.

Smith's book , an update and expansion of his earlier volume, *The World's Wasted Wealth*, largely consists of a surprising examination of wasted labor and expenditures in the American economy that might be averted with different production forms and priorities. Each chapter, organized by sector, provides both a critique and an implicit alternative. At the end of this exercise Smith tallies the amount of labor wasted in the economy and suggests that there is substantial room for moving to shorter work weeks, providing guaranteed incomes through a negative income tax, and generally making work more interesting, should a full-scale program of economic rationalization come to fruition.

A brief review of three of Smith's sectoral analyses gives a sense of his methodology and the scale of the waste he identifies.

Insurance: Smith quotes heavily two 1980s studies of the insurance industry that point out its significant waste. Due to bureaucratic requirements, the taking of profit, etc., only 45-50% of premiums collected by private insurance agencies are actually paid out in the form of claims. Yet the public Social Security system expends less than 1% of its collection on administrative and labor costs! Smith estimates that a public insurance system might be able to run most common forms of insurance with only 6% expenditure on administration; thus there is a wastage equivalent to 40% of the industry stemming from the fact that insurance is provided by a multitude of competing private groups. Smith cites several Canadian provinces that did provide state-run"social insurance" on various items beginning in the 1970s, and were able to cut rates significantly, respond to claims more generously, and still return a profit to the province coffers. Should a social insurance system be introduced in the United States (including coverage of health, life, fire, auto, etc.), Smith calculates that roughly 1.9 million people currently employed by private insurers—the salesmen and check writers—would become superfluous.

Law: Again, Smith quotes heavily from various studies and testimonies from lawyers commenting on the wastefulness and social irrationality of the current legal system, building a tally of the huge sums lawyers collect on both sides of litigation battles. Smith proposes an alternative legal system for civil matters in which lawyers would become largely superfluous, and the parties would have strong incentives to settle under the supervision of a judge. All civil suits would first be referred to a publicly paid mediator who would collect the relevant facts and attempt to propose an agreement; if that agreement fails, the case goes before a judge, who makes a decision and explains it in writing. After this judgment, the option of going to the adversarial courts with lawyers remains available "if either party feels justice has been denied."

Smith also urges the replacement of probate processes with a simple *inter vivos* trust form to eliminate the need for costly property assessments, and the development of easy-to-use public forms for most routine legal matters such as uncontested divorce, adoptions, and name changes. The potential result of these changes, Smith suggests, is that again some 1.5 million employees in the legal industry would become superfluous. Labor time now employed in a profitable but socially wasteful industry would be freed up.

Food: Smith's focus here is on wasted resources, not wasted labor. Smith strongly advocates shifting away from production of beef and other meats to a more resource-efficient grain and vegetable diet, and, like Jeremy Rifkin in *Beyond Beef* (and drawing explicitly on Francis Moore Lappe's *Diet for a Small Planet*), the author points out the huge expenditures of water and grain involved in meat production (on the scale of 840 gallons of water per steak). Smith further argues that most current world hunger could be ended if each country focused on efficient production of food for its own people, instead of organizing agriculture around export crops. Less convincing is Smith's call for an end to all U.S. agricultural exports (as the end result of a reformed world food system), which he estimates would free up over 2 million agriculture-related workers for more productive tasks.

Other sectors Smith addresses include health care, transportation, the funeral industry, and telemarketing. Smith attempts to calculate the total amount of "wasted" labor in the economy, estimating that out of 114.4 million jobs in 1989, some 37.2 million could be eliminated through reforms of the types outlined above. Dividing the remaining work by the available labor force (plus discouraged unemployed workers, homeless persons, and others not counted in official labor pool totals), Smith suggests that the work week could be reduced to 3 days, or even as few as 2.3 days.

Smith's book, although undeniably idiosyncratic, is a very substantial piece of work that compels the reader to radically alter one's view of the economy, and particularly the familiar notions of waste and efficiency. Smith's most important contribution may simply be to expose the massive waste of labor and resources in current capitalist economies. This realization provides a context in which serious discussion of economic alternatives that, although imperfect themselves, might on balance do as well or better as capitalism in efficiently utilizing labor and resources, becomes much more plausible. When it is believed that the market process *ipso facto* produces the most efficient use of resources, such a discussion of alternatives is necessarily quite constrained in its assumptions (and in fact usually never gets started).

Margrit Kennedy. *Interest and Inflation Free Money*. Philadelphia: New Society Publishers, 1995.

Kennedy, a professor of "Ecological Building Techniques" at the University of Hanover in Germany, has a strong interest in alternative forms of economics. She makes an interesting case for an elegantly simple model of "inflation-free money." Paralleling Henry George's 19th century critique of the unearned income accruing to holders of land, Kennedy notes that the same phenomenon takes places with holders of money, who can hold onto it as long as they like without fear of its losing value (unlike, say, holders of a barrel of apples). Hence, they can charge a price (interest) for the use of this money by others. The result is not only economic injustice flowing from the debtor-creditor relationship, but also wild swings in whole economies as the price of money rises (causing slowdowns) and falls (causing expansion periods). Kennedy also argues that the charging of interest drives inflation in modern economies, estimating that 50% of the cost of consumer goods in contemporary Germany consists of the cost of acquiring capital (interest).

Drawing heavily on the writings of late 19th-century German merchant Silvio Gesell, Kennedy states that the alternative to this fundamental feature of modern capitalism—the bearing of interest—is to charge fees on those who hold money in excess of what they can use. Kennedy describes an experiment in Worgl, Austria in the 1930s with a form of local currency which lost value over time. At the end of the month note holders had to pay a 1% tax on the currency, or else it would not be valid for the next month. (Each bill received a stamp each month indicating payment of the tax.) The result was a hot-potato effect that caused the newly issued money to circulate over 20 times faster than normal Schillings, resulting in a sharp decline in local unemployment. Fees collected from the monthly taxes on the money went to public expenditures. This experiment was banned by a worried Austrian National Bank, despite widespread interest in replicating the model in Austria and elsewhere.

Noting that "money" itself is a social creation, and as such capable of being changed, Kennedy uses the Worgl experiment to demonstrate the benefits of creating a form of money which does not gain value by being kept out of circulation: a short-term economic boom, longer-term economic stability as the interest rate cycle is ended, the elimination of inflation, and greater social equity over time. A modern equivalent of the Worgl experiment would be a system of "parking fees" for money. A sliding scale would be set up, whereby at the end of a given time period persons holding cash would have to pay, for instance, a 6% fee in order to continue using the cash. Those with their money in bank accounts would pay smaller fees depending on the nature of their deposit (with no fee for very long-term deposits), but banks would be responsible for paying the parking fees on those monies. Combining the parking fee idea for inflation-free money with a program of land reform (combining communal land ownership with private use, for an annual fee, a la Henry George) and tax reform (taxing products, not incomes, a sentiment in the same vein as Daly and Cobb's tax agenda) would, in Kennedy's rather optimistic view, "create an ecological economy in which goods and services could be produced at an optimum size and level of complexity because that is where they would be the cheapest, i.e. most competitive in a free system." [85] Or to put it another way, Kennedy holds the view that redesigning money plus land and tax reforms would correct and vindicate a free-market economic system.

Kennedy is persuasive in suggesting the possibilities of a different monetary system, and her idea is worthy of being piloted at a local level, as the next stage of development in local currency and time-dollar programs. Kennedy recognizes the opposition of central banking units to these kinds of schemes; the only way to build a public consensus that might overcome this opposition is to create models demonstrating the practical, positive impacts of an interest-free monetary system. Kennedy speculates that more thoroughgoing attempts at monetary reform will probably occur first in the Third World and possibly Scandinavia, although countries like the United States are ripe for local-level attempts at a modern Worgl model.

Sam Smith. *Sam Smith's Great American Political Repair Manual*. New York: W.W. Norton and Company, 1997.

As the title indicates, this entertaining and informative book is a primer for would-be grassroots activists, with an emphasis on building economic alternatives. Smith, a long-time Washington, DC activist and editor of the *Progressive Review*, peppers succinct critical analysis of contemporary American politics in down-to-earth language with plenty of practical ideas for change. While Smith does not aspire to envision an alternative system, he is strongly influenced by Daly and Cobb and shares an orientation towards building ground-up, democratic forms of economic enterprise.

Probably the most important point of the book is Smith's first one: Don't mistake the "system" for America. Smith writes that "The 'system' is not America. The 'system' is not us. It represents neither the land nor its people, neither our ideals nor our souls. One reason so many of us feel disaffected is that we know in our hearts—even if we can't think of the right words or actions—that much of what we find in the 'system' no longer matches what we believe America should be about." [86] Among the more specific points Smith offers are "A Really Simple Rule on Privatization: Ask the following question: Is this something about which citizens should have a say? If the answer is yes, don't privatize"; advice on how to run a local meeting ("Hide your copy of *Robert's Rules of Order*"); and pointed instruction for environmental activists ("Don't be a prig."). [87]

On economic affairs, Smith makes the straightforward case for rejecting balanced budgets as an economic and political priority, and endorses alternative indicators, local currencies, cooperatives, "civic enterprises," credit unions, rechartered corporations, employee ownership, shorter work weeks, and consumer boycotts. Other subjects addressed include race relations, urban design, the environmental agenda, crime, education, and how to utilize the local media (or build your own). All in all, this political repair manual lives up to its billing and succeeds in bringing something of the spirit of a "building a good society" to every page in a way that most of the other prose works noted in this bibliography do not. This book is an important resource for helping communities make a thousand flowers bloom in the near future, especially as disillusionment with the trajectory of American politics continues to grow. Any serious movement will need many more highly accessible books of this ilk.

Academic Philosophers and Political Scientists

Iris Marion Young. *Justice and the Politics of Difference*. Princeton: Princeton University Press, 1990.

Young's book opens with a critique of the "distributive paradigm" in political theories of justice, as exemplified by John Rawls and his successors. The distributive paradigm, according to Young, by focusing on the end-result distribution of goods as the substance of justice, tends to ignore or obscure the power structures—the "rules and relations"—which drive such distribution, and also wrongly assumes that all social goods can be characterized as something "possessed" by individuals. Young goes on to provide a five-featured definition of "oppression" to account more deeply for the varieties of injustice experienced in multicultural American society today. While her categories of "exploitation," "marginalization," and "powerlessness" are widely noted in both Marxist and liberal writings on justice, Young's discussion of "cultural imperialism" and "systemic violence" add new dimensions to the debate.

"Cultural imperialism," according to Young, refers to the process by which a dominant group expresses a vision of its own particularity as the "norm," negating or ignoring the cultural particularities of other groups. In the United States, this imperialism is expressed principally through the media and popular culture but also, for instance, in the assumptions guiding school and university curricula. According to Young, the liberal ideas of "impartiality" as justice and of providing a universal norm need to be replaced by conceptions of the good society which recognize the inherent differences legitimately present in various social groups (racial, religious, gender, sexual orientation, etc.).

Young caps the book by offering a vision of "city life" as a normative basis for good-society thinking that incorporates difference. Young's ideal city would be characterized by "social differentiation without exclusion," "variety," and "eroticism," that is, the potential experience of novelty. These criteria are consciously opposed to communitarian thought, which in Young's view presumes homogenous communities and potentially leads to the walling off of communities and the exclusion of undesirable groups. The "mystical" quest for "wholeness" characteristic of communitarian thought, Young urges, must simply be dropped given the realities of unique social groups in a diverse society. She further critiques advocates of a decentralized community like Bookchin for devoting inadequate attention to the problem of achieving justice—a balance of power—between communities.

For all this, however, Young's practical political program has much in common with the left wing of the communitarian movement (such as Alperovitz), and draws heavily on recent accounts of how landholding and business elites dominate urban political economy (i.e. Stephen Elkin). Young speaks favorably of the calls of Gerald Frug and others to expand municipal legal powers in order to allow cities greater direction of their own economy and to permit the municipalization of key sectors such as banking and insurance. She calls attention to the damage to the public good of privatized land use processes, including how the separation of home and work specifically damages women's lives (a point developed more fully by Dolores Hayden, Martha Ritzdorf, Leslie Weisman, and a number of other writers).

In contrast to Frug, Bookchin, and others Young's core unit of governance is not the city but the *region*, conceived as an entire metropolitan area, including central city, suburbs, and edges. A regional government, Young states, would be able to disburse public spending on schools and infrastructure equally among both city and suburbs, thus promoting justice among communities, and would serve as an effective locus for democratic planning of the economy.

While Young does not specify what degree of enterprise"socialization" would be required, she holds out the vision of "democratized regional-level decision making" in order to "end corporate monopoly of the productive capital of the region." [88] Major new investments and land use decisions would thence be made with the public good in mind, not according to the logic of private capital's needs. Young believes the substantive goals of such democratized planning should be the expansion of public spaces (parks, piazzas and the like), the promotion of "liberty" (largely by abolishing NIMBY-istic zoning codes) and the fostering of diverse neighborhoods that integrate homes, workplaces, and recreational space.

Phillipe Van Parijs. *Real Freedom For All*. Oxford: Clarendon Press, 1995.

Van Parijs, perhaps best described as a "philosophical economist," asks what it is persons who are concerned with capitalist inequalities yet also believe that liberty is the supreme political value should advocate. Van Parijs's answer is that real freedom—substantive freedom to exercise choice and self-direction over the course of one's life—would be best served by a system of guaranteed incomes, unconditionally provided and separate from whatever one earns as a worker (or capital holder). The size of this basic income should be at the maximum sustainable level a society can afford (such that it does not drain the economy of its capacity to reproduce itself).

The guaranteed income is to be financed out of general taxation, including heavy levies on wealth transfers (inheritance), and routine income taxes. Van Parijs believes the proposal is compatible with both capitalist and socialist institutions: the choice between the two systems should be on pragmatic grounds. Van Parijs' judgment is that there should be a presumption towards capitalism on efficiency grounds, but the author concedes that in some circumstances socialistic institutions can help build the cultural and social base required to support a guaranteed income proposal. (Although Van Parijs defends the right of even the person who does not work at all to receive guaranteed income, he concedes that a "you must work to eat" policy in some form may be necessary to build popular consent for the overall scheme.)

Van Parijs sees the guaranteed income proposal as very much in the tradition of—and an appropriate institutional application of—the "difference principle" articulated by John Rawls in his classic *A Theory of Justice*, which holds that the only justifiable inequalities are those in the best interest of the least well off. Having made his initial proposition, Van Parijs spends the rest of the book discussing all the possible objections, philosophical and practical, from left and right, armored with the philosophical standpoint that the substantive freedom of each and all is the supreme value.

Van Parijs' book will no doubt serve as a philosophical handbook for other intellectuals and advocates who favor the basic income notion. The book does suffer, however, from Van Parijs' omission of estimates of just how large the "maximum sustainable income" would actually be in Europe or the United States today, although it is quite clear that Van Parijs believes it will be, in most circumstances, enough to provide a decent living apart from one's wage income.

It should also be noted that Van Parijs is the Secretary of the Basic Income European Network, an international consortium of dozens of social policy thinkers and politicians advocating the guaranteed income idea in public and academic arenas. Among the prominent social thinkers involved in the network are Dutch scholar Robert J. van der Veen, Claus Offe, and French scholar Marie-Louise Duboin. Duboin, in particular, has developed an argument for distributing our common technological "inheritance" in the form of a basic income, a line of reasoning strikingly similar to that of Gar Alperovitz.

Joshua Cohen and Joel Rogers

Associations and Democracy, New York: Verso, 1995.
"Associative Democracy" in Bardhan and Roemer, eds. *Market Socialism*. New York: Oxford University Press, 1993.

Cohen and Rogers have forwarded the "associative strategy" as a way to "[advance the] commitment" to increased equality they share with market socialists within the context of a capitalist property regime (although they allow that the associative approach and redistributing ownership rights could go hand in hand). Simply put, the idea of "associative" democracy is to develop nongovernmental organizational forms that act on behalf of specific constituencies. The result is not only better representation (thereby counteracting the influences of organized business on the political process), but also the possibility of these organizations assisting government in executing policy. Unions, employer groups, advocacy organizations, and volunteer groups are examples of "associations."

"Our central contention is that in any large-scale modern society, stable approximation to egalitarian democratic norms requires a high level of secondary group organization of a certain kind," Cohen and Rogers argue in their contribution to the Bardhan and Roemer volume.

...Using conventional tools of public policy (taxes, subsidies, legal sanctions), as applied through the familiar decision-making procedures of formal government (legislatures and administrative bodies, as overseen by the courts), it proposes associative reform to address each of the sources of frustration just noted. Where inequalities in political representation exist, it recommends efforts to promote the organized

154

representation of excluded interests. Where group particularism undermines democratic deliberation or popular sovereignty, it recommend efforts to encourage the organized to be more other-regarding in their actions. And, perhaps most immediately, where associations have greater capacity than the state for promoting democratic ends, or where their participation could improve the effectiveness of government programs, it recommends encouraging a more central role for groups in public governance. In this last we wish to break out of the states-and-market framework that continues to captivate most discussion of public governance, and that is particularly disabling for egalitarians long identified exclusively with statist strategies of reform.[89]

After defending this idea against the traditional charge from democratic theorists of "factionalism," Cohen and Rogers suggest how "associative reform" might be applied to labor relations in the United States. State power would be used to make unionization easier, to "raise the social wage," to develop forms of worker organization for non-unionized workers, and to create institutions that simultaneously centralize wage bargaining and decentralize bargaining on work conditions. To support this agenda, government could rewrite the rules on union organizing, create legal provisions for multiemployer bargaining, and mandate shop committees in both union and nonunion plants. The end result, they argue, "would make U.S. industrial relations substantially more workable and more congruent with democratic ideals." [90]

Cohen and Rogers extend this idea beyond labor representation to other collaborations. They discuss how vocational training might be improved through partnerships between employer associations and unions to define vocational standards and carry out the training (with the assistance of public money). Workplace committees also might be empowered to carry out self-monitoring of safety practices as an alternative to a sporadic system of state OSHA inspections. Cohen and Rogers also believe the general approach might be extended beyond its obvious application in workplace issues to income policy and environmental problems.

Clearly this approach is not a call for a new system, but rather a new strategy for how progressives can make do within the current one. Indeed the authors dismiss market socialist ideas not so much as undesirable but as politically farfetched. (Yet their own labor agenda, much of which has long been the agenda of organized labor, does not have any obvious political viability in the visible future either.) Still, Cohen and Rogers add to the debate by pointing out the role which organized nongovernmental groups must play in the practical governance of any system, no matter what the property regime, and by pointing out ways the state might actively encourage "civil society." Further work might explore the capacity of the emergent community-based economics movement—consisting mostly of non-governmental organizations such as land trusts, community development corporations, cooperatives—to facilitate public governance in an alternative political and economic regime (including, importantly, the transition to a different system).

E.M. Adams. *A Society Fit For Human Beings*. Albany: SUNY Press, 1997.

Adams, a philosophy professor at the University of North Carolina, offers a critique of contemporary American civilization from a "realistic humanist" perspective. From the standpoint of developing human beings who are inner-directed, able to develop their capacities, and capable of pursuing a rational life plan, American society is failing. (This theme is not unique—it is a hallmark, for instance, of the work of neo-Aristotelian philosopher Martha Nussbaum.) Adams argues that contemporary American society is fundamentally organized around the principles of wealth acquisition and military power, which in turn implies a glorification of scientific and technological development at the expense of human values, or even self-understanding. The result is a culture that "fails most fundamentally."

Adams writes that "the modern conception of knowledge and the worldview generated by our dominant cultural perspective undermine the humanistic foundations of human identity, society, and the whole culture, even science and the technological enterprises on which our wealth and power depend. Clearly something is radically wrong." [91]

After fleshing out the "realistic humanist view" further, Adams proceeds by analyzing different components of society and describing what they would look like in a healthy, humanistic-based society, starting with individual character, and going on to include the family, the local community, education, economics, government and civic life, the military, and religion. The discussion is rich in each of these areas, and Adams can be reasonably read as being quite "conservative" in his appraisal of the importance of character development and family life. However, the area of most relevance to this study—and the acknowledged key to the whole puzzle—is Adams' thinking on what an alternative economic system that does meet humanistic standards would look like.

Adams pulls no punches in describing the need for a different system: "Unlike the welfare state that tries to put something of a humanistic face on the materialistic economy by external legal means, humanization of the economy would build humanistic values and ways of thought into the very constitution and practices of the economy itself. This would be such a radical transformation of our present system that the very thought of it is daunting. It would be the end of capitalism." Adams favors first reorienting the very purpose of the economy: "The economy should not be thought of primarily as society's way of organizing and managing the production and distribution of goods and services...The economy should be thought of as our primary way of organizing and managing our creative and productive work in meeting human needs. When thought of in this way, meaningful, self-fulfilling work is taken to be one of the human needs that the economy must meet." [92]

Taking off from this last point, Adams would restructure enterprises so that employees were no longer simply wage laborers but "partners" in the enterprise. Partners would have full job security, a voice in how the enterprise is run, and ownership shares. While still operating within a consumer market, Adams would have these enterprises govern themselves internally, with maximum emphasis on providing meaningful work for all—that is on treating all employees as worthy human beings with their own developmental needs. Even menial work, framed within the context of community purpose and bestowed with dignity, can be fulfilling, Adams suggests. Similarly, Adams would have the enterprises (and their investors) be concerned that their products are socially useful, of real value to consumers and society.

> ...[T]he ideal of a humanistic economy would be one in which all the participants would have positions in which they could function as full-fledged human beings and find a measure of self-fulfillment in the performance of their responsibilities. There would not be the same effort to keep the monetary cost of production down, nor the same effort to keep monetary profits as high. And profits would not be sought from trivial or harmful goods and services. But the situation might not be as bad for monetary profits as it might appear. With genuine identification with their jobs, satisfaction in their work, and high morale, workers would no doubt be highly productive.

Such an economy of course could not sustain itself unless embedded in a culture committed to humanistic values, Adams stresses. "If the people judged themselves, others, and the institutions of society in terms of humanistic values, then self-interest and social pressures would reinforce humanistic ways of thought and behavior. Economic enterprises that tried to function by capitalist values would be in ill repute and unsupported by the employees and by the public." [93]

In addition to this humanistic private sector, Adams reserves a strong role for nonprofits and public institutions and condemns much of the current wave of privatization of public services.

Clearly, this proposal has much in common with labor-cooperative based visions of market socialism, and perhaps even more with advocates of "socially responsible business" (such as environmentalists Paul Hawken and Hazel Henderson). While it would be premature to judge that a system of quasi-private enterprises that pursue profits within bounds limited by respect for humanistic criteria is theoretically impossible, it is difficult to imagine the cultural revolution needed to bring about such a "change in the bottom line" taking place without directly changing the power base of the economic institutions.

In terms of the vision itself, compared to direct community ownership strategies, Adams's hope to reconcile a market system with humanistic values seems at best a halfway house and is probably unstable structurally (unless steps were taken to deliberately reduce competitive pressures on the enterprises). Still, the vision Adams forwards is a plausible description of what "private" enterprise under a mixed economy that had a community ownership structure at is core might look like.

Beyond the pros and cons of Adams's thoughts on economics, his book provides a valuable service in approaching the "system" question from the other end of the problem: Instead of starting with discussion about abstract systems, Adams starts by developing a lofty vision of what a healthy, self-governing human character looks like, and proceeds upwards from there. In some respects, starting at this end of the problem—rooting one's analysis in a grounded conception of what human beings are for—guarantees a more radical conclusion than beginning with political ideology. (Wendell Berry is another noted practitioner of this type of thinking.)

Additionally, the similarities between Adams's views of the good society and that of other, very different, thinkers covered in this bibliography are noteworthy. Though equally erudite, one could not imagine books written with more different styles, different parlances, and different assumptions than

Adams's *Society Fit for Human Beings* and say, Rudolf Bahro's *The Alternative in Eastern Europe* or Albert and Hahnel's *Looking Forward*. Yet all three books have much in common as to the substantive vision of what goes on in the everyday life of the good society, particularly the goal of fulfilling work. The similarities suggest a certain consensus of vision among contemporary thinkers as to what a good society should look like, even though these writers often have radically different starting points of analysis, and drastically differing views on how such a society could or should fit together institutionally.

John Dryzek. *Democracy in Capitalist Times*. Oxford: Oxford University Press, 1996.

Dryzek, who previously published several books noting the inadequacy of existing mechanisms of democratic social choice for achieving ecological rationality, here turns to the question of democracy per se. Noting how current forms of democracy are based on an aggregation-of-preferences model in which political actors compete in the democratic arena to maximize their private aims, (as opposed to "deliberative democracy," which is based on public argument over how to forward the public good), Dryzek in this text despairs of the prospects for achieving substantial democratization of the state—or of overturning capitalism. In his concluding section, Dryzek poses the questions as follows: "Should the end in view [for forwarding a deliberative democracy agenda] be postcapitalist democracy or democracy remaining in the shadow of the capitalist state? Are these two ends mutually exclusive?" [94]

Dryzek examines and finds wanting a number of theories that pin hopes for democracy on a move beyond capitalism. Taking over state power within the context of a capitalist economy is not an advisable strategy, given the constraints of the current system: "Disaffected populism seeks to enter and capture the state, but that is a higher-risk strategy, for any movement that succeeds in its efforts here becomes subject to all the state imperatives that are so destructive to democracy." [95] That is, populists can only achieve their goals by running roughshod over the idea of deliberative democracy. (Dryzek fails to note that this objection may not deter many populists, especially those right of center.)

The history of revolutionary change is similarly discouraging as a model for moving towards a deepened democracy; Dryzek writes that "The normal response by postrevolutionary states, irrespective of their ideology, is a centralization of authority that by definition hurts the prospects for democracy of any sort." [96] Nor is waiting for the ecologically induced demise of capitalism a hopeful strategy; for one thing, one might be waiting quite a long time, "and more important, the outcome of any such denouement is uncertain. Convulsion will not necessarily produce a more democratic political economy." Speaking of the "imaginative" school of democracy advocates in general, Dryzek argues that "The trouble is that these [proposals for a different society] are often inattentive to practical constraints and possibilities; they are idealist as opposed to realist and as such are not well placed to contribute to the real-world conversation of democratic development." [97]

Hence, according to Dryzek, the best hope for forwarding democratic aims in the near future is in civil society initiatives, within the context of capitalism, that do not aim at the direct takeover of state power. Advocates of democracy should "adopt a radicalism that involves permanent confrontation with the state," and that aims to create new public discourses that are intrinsically democratic and that shift the parameters in which state policies are enacted. Classic examples of this form of democratization outside the state include the ecological movement and contemporary feminism; Dryzek additionally cites the emergence of an international community of nongovernmental organizations which have used United Nations summits and other worldwide gatherings to shape public consciousness on ecological matters and other issues. Dryzek also rightly calls for close attention to the content of new political discourses and the power of the discourse in itself to shape public perceptions (a fact not lost on Newt Gingrich or the Republican Party in general since the 1980s).

Dryzek's critique of "idealist" literature, including many of the texts discussed in this bibliography, surely has merit. Yet he fails to recognize that the point about connecting ideas with practical realities is far from lost on many writers who at the same time forward a vision of the good society. Nor does he carry the point about establishing public discourses to the entirely defensible conclusion that in the contemporary situation, good society-talk can establish a new discursive space capable of stimulating the public's political imagination and providing a common framework to energize and sustain practical work over time. More to the point, Dryzek leaves the reader with only a politics of resistance; yet common complaints among those who actually do resistance-style political work are, "What is it we are really for?" and "Is there a light at the end of the tunnel?" It is a mistake to try to read the normative question out of the equation by validating only practical struggles as important, as if the normative question never enters into day-to-day practical struggles, or, to reiterate, as if fresh public discourse might not change and expand what is possible now.

Finally, the possibility of evolutionary reconstruction of basic political and economic institutions is simply not on Dryzek's radar screen. Such an approach would start not with capture of national-level state power but with the steady development of alternative economic institutions and supporting state policies which in turn help shape new cultural and political norms (including, centrally, a new public discourse) that ultimately might enable the reshaping of larger-scale institutions (See the Alperovitz annotation for a description of this conception.) This reconstructive path, whatever its ultimate feasibility in the new century, at least stands a better a chance of upholding and expanding the norms of democratic public discourse than either the "populist" or the "revolutionary" models of change which Dryzek rightly criticizes.

Thomas Naylor and William H. Willimon. *Downsizing the USA.* Grand Rapids, MI: Wm. B. Eerdmans Publishing Co., 1997.

Naylor and Willimon review many of the dysfunctions and absurdities of contemporary American society, with special emphasis on educational institutions, and apply in a thoroughgoing fashion a single proposed remedy: shrink the scale of the country and its major institutions to a more a manageable, livable size. "What we are proposing is decentralizing, downsizing, and dissolving virtually every major institution in American and replacing these obsolete monoliths with collections of small, voluntary, cooperative communities, developed entirely through bottom-up participatory means." [98] Just as some large corporations, finding their own operations too far flung and unwieldy, have downsized into smaller operations, so the government apparatus of the United States as a whole should be broken down into a series of regional governments. Naylor and Willimon also mount an argument for steadily building down America's largest cities by moving urban dwellers into small, dying rural towns that need more people.

Frequently citing the culture and quality of life of tiny Vermont as a positive example, Naylor and Willimon envision a nation with power once again invested in small communities, operating within smaller state units. They do not directly tackle the question of corporate power and economic ownership—that is, what the underlying architecture of power in the reinvigorated local communities will be—other than to favor breaking up the largest corporations into more place-based, smaller-scale businesses and to endorse the expansion of locally owned sustainable businesses (as found so often in Vermont!). Naylor and Willimon, who cite Gandhi's ideas of small villages that own their own land collectively, would clearly be sympathetic to efforts to directly root capital in specific places through community or worker ownership, but their concern is not with reconstructing a different economic system.

The authors mount a variety of arguments for their core regionalization proposal, some more convincingly than others: smaller-scale countries tend to have better economic records than larger-scale countries; the powerful "megastate" crushes diversity, initiative, and variety of life; a continent-sized government cannot be democratic; top-down solutions to problems like racial inequality in the South have proven inadequate without bottom-up community change; the differences of interest and demographics among different regions is much wider than usually assumed; a series of regional governments would allow greater room for innovation; African-Americans and other minorities could attain more meaningful political clout, perhaps even majority status in some areas, if the country were broken up; there is no sense of national community adequate to support national-level federal-style liberalism; dependence on the federal government has left local-scale institutions powerless and inert; large-scale bureaucratic institutions in areas like health care and social welfare are dehumanizing and often ineffective; the large size of the United States forces some states to subsidize activities in other states (like Colorado taxes going to support Amtrak) from which they do not benefit. (On this last score, it might be conversely pointed out that national-scale government prevents some regions from implementing programs that would benefit their own states. For instance, the mid-Atlantic states would surely prefer a higher level of Amtrak funding from the federal government than the effective opposition of many Western state senators allows.)

Naylor and Willimon devote particular attention to the problem of dismantling the military-industrial complex as a precondition for substantial decentralization, and they also take up some of the constitutional and practical issues arising from a state or set of states choosing to formally break away. In fact, Naylor and Willimon go even further than other advocates of new regional governments such as Alperovitz: Not content simply to move the bulk of government operations to regional units, they envision out-and-out secession by various states. (Alaska could secede, and become responsible for its own defense.) The authors also are willing to see not just six or eight but perhaps many more distinct governance units in the United States.

While the thrust of Naylor and Willimon's very provocative book is quite compelling, this last point leads to two reservations: First, it seems unlikely in the extreme that a state would choose to remove itself from the power of the American military. A politically plausible strategy for decentralization will probably have to decouple the regionalization of domestic governance functions from security questions, at least in the near term. Second, the authors do not take up the question of whether certain small states—if not Vermont, than perhaps Arkansas—are simply too small to attain economic independence and self-sufficiency. Could Arkansas really sell enough timber and export enough chicken meat to buy all the goods it needs to import? Such states might be better off acting in a concert of states, that is, a regional alliance. To be sure, Naylor and Willimon allow for such alliances, but while the authors are quite clear in stating that some sizes are too big, they underplay the converse possibility, that some sizes of government could be too small to function well.

Nancy Fraser. *Justice Interruptus: Critical Reflections on the "Postsocialist" Condition*. New York: Routledge, 1997.

Left feminist Nancy Fraser here provides a series of essays on gender politics within a "postindustrial context." Of greatest interest to this bibliography is a chapter entitled "After the Family Wage: A Postindustrial Thought Experiment," in which she presents a highly persuasive "complex" account of what full-fledged gender equity would really entail, and critiques existing social democratic/liberal feminist strategies for promoting equality as inadequate. The result is a seminal discussion of why welfare state strategies that do not seek to alter the patterns of both men's and women's lives cannot produce a society in which men and women share genuine equality.

Fraser lays out seven conditions a society must meet if it is to realize equality between men and women. First, no one should be in poverty; second, women should be freed from "exploitable dependence" on husbands, employers, or the state; third, women should be paid as well as men; fourth, women should have as much leisure time and rest as men; fifth, women should receive the same respect as men, particularly women who act as caregivers (to children, the elderly, etc.); sixth, the domestic sphere should not be shut off from spheres of work and public life, leading to the marginalization of those who give care; and seventh, masculine norms regarding lifestyle , workplace roles, and the like should be "de-centered," and traits now associated with women revalued.

Fraser then shows how the "universal breadwinner" model, aimed at opening up women's access to well-remunerated employment, could only partly meet the conditions of real gender equality. This strategy, which Fraser associates with American liberal feminists, envisions a system in which quality day care is available universally, workplaces are reformed to accommodate women's full participation, and women's pay vis-a-vis men is substantially increased via the "comparable worth" model. Social insurance covers those who cannot work. The overall goal is, through full-employment policies, to enable all women (and men) to earn enough money to support themselves and a family. Fraser credits this strategy as a credible way to end female poverty and exploitation, but argues that this approach cannot meet the other five conditions of complex gender equity.

The model is particularly inadequate with respect to leisure time: women who cannot afford to hire servants or convince husbands to help at home, or who are single, are likely to get caught holding the domestic work bag alone, on top of their paid work. As Fraser notes, "Anyone who does not free-ride in this possible postindustrial world is likely to be harried and tired." Moreover, the model valorizes traditional male models of the breadwinner whose role, utterly separate from the domestic sphere, is to earn money for dependents. Paid work is given ultimate value for men and women, and unpaid work is seen as less important or valuable. This model is unacceptable, in Fraser's view.

A second approach, labeled by Fraser the "Caregiver-Parity Model," and associated with European welfare states, is to make the transitions between work and caregiving roles characteristic of many women's lives costless. In addition to standard social welfare provisions, generous allowances for pregnancy and maternity leave and guarantees to protect women's job security and seniority would characterize this approach. The idea is to enable women to move back and forth between work and caregiving roles as seamlessly as possible. Again, Fraser sees this model as inadequate. First, workplaces would now be seen to have two sharply defined tracks, the still-normative masculine careerist track, and the "mommy" track. Women would still be marginalized in the workplace, and apt to earn lower wages, since job

164

advancement would be slower for those who alternated between work and caregiving. (Two-income families could conceivably choose to have both partners on the "mommy track," but probably would not for financial reasons.)

Fraser is careful to note that both models are politically implausible at the present time, but her larger point is that both are also inadequate as a vision of a society in which men and women could be equal. She briefly sketches a third option that aims not at adjusting women's lives and roles to the norm of a male breadwinner, but rather at changing life patterns of both men and women so that both shared in work and caregiving roles. Both men and women are to participate in all spheres of society. This would mean not only full social insurance provisions and workplaces that assumed that all workers had domestic roles to play, but also reduced work hours. The idea is to directly challenge the inherited norm of work life in postindustrialized societies, and, in the process, to deconstruct inherited norms regarding gender. As Fraser puts it, "The trick is to imagine a social world in which citizens' lives integrate wage earning, caregiving, community activism, political participation, and involvement in the associational life of civil society—while also leaving time for some fun." [99]

Obviously, this model also faces the problem of political implausibility, much like the scenarios of expanded social democracy discussed in chapter one of this bibliography. Moreover, Fraser has not thoroughly sketched out all the conditions in which a fully egalitarian model of gender equity would take root: For instance, in addition to workplace reform, universal social provisions, and shorter work weeks, a geographical redesign of communities to more closely locate work, home, and market would also be needed to break down the dichotomy between private and public spheres (as pointed out by Alperovitz as well as numerous feminist writers on city design). Such redesign in turn requires greater community control over land use decisions at the local level. That idea, combined with Fraser's own observations that public control over corporations, higher taxes on income and wealth, and public direction of investment would also be needed to make a revived "welfare state" workable, suggests that ultimately an egalitarian model of gender relations would depend on a thorough reconstruction of the institutional bases of capitalist political economies. While Fraser has yet to speak to the question of building an effective strategy to effect such change, she is quite clear in expressing what a vision of gender equality entails, and quite correct to conclude that "unless we are guided by this vision now, we will never get any closer to achieving it."

Harold Wells. *A Future for Socialism? Political Theology and the "Triumph of Capitalism."* Valley Forge, PA: Trinity Press International, 1996.

This book is a conscientious search on the part of a serious Christian with socialist inclinations to evaluate whether, and in what form, "socialist" politics might remain a viable option for Christian commitment in the context of contemporary North American politics. "The task of Christian political theology, as I am using the term here, is not to speak in vague abstractions and generalities about the political order. Rather, it is to clarify political options for Christians as followers of Jesus Christ." After expressing his sympathies for the emphasis of liberation theology on embracing the poor and challenging capitalism, Wells takes the decisive step, beyond simply stating value preferences, into concrete social analysis: "Theological reflection upon social systems and political ideologies may not remain at an abstract, ethereal level. It must take account of and interact with the empirical realities that are described and analyzed by historians and social scientists. That is why our theological reflections must now move in the direction of socio-analytic and, especially, historical considerations." [100]

Wells then commences with a critical history of the major 20th century versions of "socialism," including the Soviet Union, pre-Marxist utopian socialists, Marx himself, the American social gospel tradition, Fabian socialism, Canadian and Scandinavian social democracy, Euro- communism, Chinese communism, independent Third World communism (Cuba, Angola), African socialism, Yugoslavian worker self-management, cooperativism in Britain and the United States, and modern day "communitarianism" (including, for instance, community land trusts). Wells also delivers a (rather conventional) critique of North American capitalism, and more devastatingly, an assessment of the impact of capitalism on the Third World. This is obviously quite a lot of ground to cover, but Wells does so succinctly and even-handedly; "the story [of socialism] is neither all gloomy nor all shining and bright," Wells tells us. Wells concludes this section of the book by approvingly quoting the last paragraph of Richard Barnet and John Cavanagh's *Global Dreams*: "Local citizens' movements and alternative institutions are springing up all over the world to meet basic economic needs, to preserve local traditions, religious life, cultural life, biological species. ... The great question of our age is whether people, acting with the spirit, energy and urgency our collective crisis requires, can develop a democratic global consciousness rooted in authentic local communities." [101] These strategies,

Wells states, "deserve the widespread support of Christian people and the churches..."

For all his fine analysis of various socialist proposals and movements past and present, Wells does not quite solve the problem of what a contemporary Christian socialist should be for—other than to forcefully state that the "socialist" idea must not be abandoned. Wells adds the following appropriately Niebhurian caveats that are de rigueur for contemporary left theologians but well worth repeating:

> No political ideology or system, not even socialism, can be absolutized or divinized by Christians. Every ideology and every political program, including every socialist one, is open to critique and revision in light of the lordship of Jesus Christ and in light of its practical contribution to the universal 'community of friends.' Nor can Christian faith be defined exclusively in terms of any particular political commitment. Yet Christian are called...to be hopeful and faithful stewards for the growth of God's Reign in the world...This means, in our global context, that capital is not 'lord.' At the same time we have to remain soberly realistic about the limitations of human achievement in history. Further, such commitment means that Christians will have to operate out of particular social analyses and strategies, i.e., they will have to live and act in accordance with some explicit, particular political-ideological stance.[102]

Wells thus clearly points to the need to develop *some* alternative: "It is common, it is politically correct, and indeed it is almost universal among theologians to deplore capitalism; but unfortunately such denunciation is rarely accompanied by the annunciation of a socialist alternative." Wells, as his endorsement of the bottom-up communitarian movement illustrates, does have a sense of where he wants to go; his cry for a fully-developed alternative illustrates a welcome receptiveness among North American theologians for a "system" proposal that connects current bottom-up movements to long-term nuts-and-bolts institutional changes. By pushing the debate beyond vague theological judgements to connect theology with practical systemic analysis, Wells makes a tremendous contribution, and serves notice that North American theological voices might yet reclaim an important role in finding new ways to challenge and transcend the "system."

Gary Dorrien. *Soul in Society*. Philadelphia: Fortress Press, 1995.

Like Wells's *A Future for Socialism?*, Gary Dorrien's *Soul in Society* is a major attempt to approach the "system problem" from the vantage point of Christian theology. Dorrien, an Episcopal priest who has previously written impressive intellectual histories of 20th-century Christian socialist thought, secular socialist thought in the United States, and postwar American neoconservatism, here provides an authoritative discussion of the "social gospel" tradition in American theology in the 20th century. While the initial material, from Troeltsch to Rauschenbusch to Reinhold Niebuhr (given here a detailed, critical assessment), is well-worn territory, Dorrien breaks new ground with his thorough discussion of trends in American Protestant theology since the 1960s (including liberation theology, feminist theology, black theology, and religious neoconservatism).

The last two chapters of Dorrien's book are of primary relevance to the system question. In his chapter on the "Economics of Democracy and the Economics of Nature," Dorrien appraises market socialism, the Meidner plan to transfer capital assets to worker's pension funds in Sweden, cooperatives in the United States, ecotheology, and the "third way" economics (closely tied to "process theology") of John Cobb.

Dorrien would like to see a rich mix of cooperative economic institutions evolve in the United States, and he suggests that this is the most appropriate strategy for progressive political forces to embrace in the coming period. Dorrien is particularly impressed with the Mondragon cooperative system in the Basque region of Spain and the rapid increase in employee-owned firms in the United States. To his credit, Dorrien does not pretend that worker firms alone are the answer.

> The kind of economic development that does not harm the earth's environment will require a dramatically expanded cooperative sector consisting of worker-owned firms that are rooted in communities, committed to survival, and prepared to accept lower returns. But it will also require more than a strategy of expanding the cooperative sector...

> Worker ownership of stock is an important but, by itself, insufficient basis for economic democracy, first because pure worker ownership often prevents cooperatives from accumulating a capital base, and second because the idea of social and economic democracy is to organize society for the sake of the common good, not just for the sake of wage earners. Economic democracy in its wider form therefore features not only

168

worker-owned cooperatives but also various forms of mutual fund or public bank social ownership that entail significant democratically determined public control of investment and decision making. ... The objective is not to eliminate property rights but to expand property rights under new forms. The mix could include national development banks, cooperative banks, employee stock ownership plans, mutual fund enterprises, community land trusts, and regional planning agencies that guide investments into locally defined areas of need, such as housing, soft-energy hardware, infrastructure maintenance, and mass transit.[103]

This is as close as Dorrien comes to a programmatic recommendation for progressive politics (and theology) to embrace in the next period—he does not see a "systemic" answer on the horizon. Yet this is clearly enough to suggest a strong direction—a direction that is quite similar to the recommendations of Wells and the outlook of several other thinkers noted in this bibliography.

In his critical discussion of Daly and Cobb and his concluding chapter assessing the capacity of mainline Protestantism to contribute to a rejuvenation and reconstruction of democratic political-economic institutions, Dorrien sees more roadblocks and obstacles ahead than reason for optimism. (Such questions as "If America is to become a community of communities dedicated to social justice and sustainable living, what are the sources or traditions of moral value that might inspire this countercultural project and enable it to gather strength?" and "Are Americans so drenched in the consumption-oriented culture of narcissism that their inherited moral languages have become unreal, unknown, or in any case unusable?" will produce more furrowed brows than quick answers from most readers.) [104] Dorrien clearly believes that in the United States the social gospel tradition is probably the most likely source of any such rejuvenation—"Mainline Christianity is far from the soul in the socialist movement that Rauschenbusch hoped it would become, but it is still the largest part of America's organized progressive political constituency." But he counters this view with several sobering observations about the weakness and decline of a mainline Protestantism that has shrunk both in numbers and also in its capacity to seriously challenge the core values of the bulk of its members. If the church is the bedrock of the American left, that suggests more about the organizational weakness of the secular "left" in America than about the strength of progressive Christianity, Dorrien's comments suggest.

Nor should Christianity be reduced to a progressive political ideology, Dorrien warns, after discussing a number of contemporary views of what the church should be in America (including Robert Bellah, Stanley Hauerwas, and James Gustafson; he is most sympathetic to the latter's notion of "participant Christianity"). And yet, if one is serious about going forward with either a progressive agenda or acting out a social gospel understanding of Christian ethics, than there can be no giving up. Dorrien thus offers the following bonus caveat for Christians who believe that God will finish what human beings cannot in the struggle for justice:

> No one knows whether America's current experiments in ecojustice and economic democracy can create new possibilities in a society driven by seemingly uncontrollable economic forces. No one can say for certain that worker and social ownership will bring about greater equality, that environmental catastrophe will be averted, or that the movements for racial and gender equality have any reasonable chance of success in a world economy that destroys nature and community. But the necessity of struggling for equality and sustainable community is certain. . . and after all our efforts to change the world are finished, it is God who will make something new in the world...[105]

Michael Lerner. *The Politics of Meaning*. New York: Addison-Wesley, 1996.

No religiously based progressive has received greater public attention in this decade than Jewish thinker and activist Michael Lerner, editor of *Tikkun* magazine. Lerner's concept of a "politics of meaning" directly challenges the ethos of "selfishness" he sees as pervasive in contemporary society. The goal, in Lerner's view, is to create a "new bottom line" for evaluating social arrangements: how well they contribute to the development and flourishing of psychologically healthy, ethically sensitive persons living meaningful lives. This conception is based on a critique of American society as failing to meet the deepest human needs for community and connection, living a purposeful life, feeling valued and respected by others, and so forth—a failure that is felt, deeply, even by persons whose paychecks are adequate enough.

From this starting point, Lerner has several pertinent observations regarding the failure of political liberalism in the past generation. Liberals, Lerner charges, have often too narrowly focused on economic issues and economic injustice, and in the process sent the message to middle-class whites that their problems—the psychological pain felt even in the lives of the well-off—aren't really that important. Conservatives, on the other hand, understood the psychological dimension of politics and crafted a narrative based on nationalist pride and upholding traditional values which spoke to voters' need for meaning. Until progressives construct a politics that transcends traditional rights-based liberalism and speaks to the wholeness of life experience, they will continue only as a spent political force in American life, and either conservatism or "cynicism" will prevail. Using a similar reasoning process, Lerner provides an interesting chapter repudiating identity politics called "Giving White Males a Break," which argues that dividing the world into camps of "oppressors" and the "oppressed" will have a negative labeling effect on those who are told they fall into the "oppressors" camp. If young, straight white males are repeatedly told they are supposed to be "oppressors," they may believe it and start acting that way. The alternative to identity politics must be one of inclusive community that recognizes the extent to which everyone in society—to varying degrees—is both harmed by and complicit in a deficient social system.

In his closing chapters, Lerner spells out his view of how economic life could support a "politics of meaning" vision—a vision of a society "in which people typically act as though they care about one another." Lerner calls for making strong neighborhoods and local communities the locus of economic life, via a regional planning mechanism that targets investment towards specific communities. Larger scale bureaucracies, whether public or private, should be broken up; and communities should be built on the ideal of achieving maximal self-sufficiency. Lerner does not spell out precisely how this goal is to be achieved, stating that both top-down and bottom-up strategies are plausible to him. Nor does he say whether the new economic units are to be public or private, or in some combination, preferring to claim a stance of "agnosticism" on the question of whether a new system should be capitalist or not. Lerner does propose a network of local and regional public development banks to target investment; national taxes on pollution and use of natural resources; the development of trade agreements incorporating environmental standards; an end to subsidies for job relocations, and so forth. (More recently, Lerner has proposed a "Social Responsibility Initiative" which would require corporations to meet numerous ethical criteria as a condition for retaining a charter to do business.)

Citing the positive example of the work motivation seen in the Israeli kibbutzim, Lerner is particularly concerned to reconstruct work life, based on three kibbutz-based principles: democratic governance at work, job rotations, and a sabbatical year for all workers similar to that already given tenured university professors. In the long run, Lerner believes significant reductions of the work week would be desirable. In any case, unlike some movements of the 1960s, Lerner insists a successful progressive movement will have to respect work and make the creation of healthy, meaningful work a central priority.

However, Lerner intends that his proposals not simply replicate those of other left thinkers: What needs to be put upfront is the goal of a society in which people care for one another, and a rejection of the cultural assumption—the "ethos of selfishness"—of atomized individuals each making contracts and cutting deals for himself. Cooperation is to be valued as an end in itself. A society in which there was stronger community, more trust, and more nurturing might plausibly hope to cut back on work now aimed simply at extracting labor effort from recalcitrant, embittered employees or providing security from crime for homes and workplaces.

Lerner goes on to sketch how an ethos of caring approach might be applied to education, family policy, and health care, before taking up in an explicit fashion the "here to there" question. Lerner offers a number of ideas, from creating a $500 tax credit for donations to nonprofits to creating "occupational stress" groups in which workers could talk about their lives to straightforward policy measures. Lerner places particular weight on the value of small study groups in consciousness-raising, and in creating a safe space for open expression of spirituality alongside political action. While any number of strategies might advance the long-term goal, in Lerner's view the primary, overriding goal is to create a spirit of hopefulness such that "all kinds of people who imagined themselves as isolated see themselves as potentially powerful." [106] The overriding spirit of cynicism and "nothing-can-be-done" in the general culture must be confronted head on; the hardest work is in once again making talk of a society based on caring and human sharing acceptable and reasonable in the larger political culture. Lerner estimates this means struggling to build a movement involving in some way a few million people, a critical mass sufficient to be a lasting force in American culture and politics.

Lerner's final chapter analyzing the short-lived embrace of the "politics of meaning" idea by Hillary Clinton is essentially a meditation and attack upon the media assumption that human beings and politicians can only be motivated by self-interest. In contrast to conventional media wisdom, Lerner insists that millions of working and middle class Americans would be receptive to a movement and a politics that spoke openly of a sense of the common good, if its advocates were serious, credible, and willing to stand up to criticism and exercise leadership instead of determining strategy based on opinion polls.

Ulrich Duchrow. *Alternatives to Global Capitalism: Drawn from Biblical History, Designed for Political Action.* Utrecht, The Netherlands: International Books, 1995.

Duchrow, a church activist and economist active in the European ecumenical movement, here provides an impressive attempt to come to terms with worldwide capitalism from a Christian perspective. In the first part of the book, Duchrow provides a critique of capitalism, with particular attention to negative environmental trends, the gap between the North and the South, and the unnecessary human suffering generated by massive inequalities. In the second part, Duchrow examines what biblical tradition has to say about economic life, drawing on both Hebrew Bible sources such as Leviticus 25 and the egalitarian impulses of the New Testament texts, and takes mainline denominations in both the United States and Europe to task for not living up to the best of this tradition or fully recognizing the ethical challenge it poses to capitalism. Duchrow then goes on to spell out practical strategies for enacting a long-term transformation of the global political and economic system.

Duchrow, who draws heavily on Daly and Cobb's *For the Common Good* as well as continental thinkers, endorses a practice of "networked small-scale alternatives" combined with political pressure aimed at existing multilateral institutions. Duchrow reviews existing local-level alternatives taking place in civil society, including Christian base intentional communities in Europe, local economic trading systems, microcredit programs, networks of socially responsible business, worker ownership, alternative technologies, and community-based banks. Duchrow also urges church institutions in particular to take a lead in abandoning hierarchical pay scales for its employees. Curiously, Duchrow at no point connects this panoply of civil society-based alternatives with policy mechanisms to strengthen them, and he bypasses entirely public ownership, at either the local or national level, as an acceptable alternative. Instead, Duchrow focuses on the potential of networking of existing alternative institutions as the basis for "political action" that directly challenges capitalist interests; Duchrow is clearly

173

cheered by the recent emergence of a strong international community of nongovernmental organizations who have turned recent United Nations Summits into fora for communicating basic democratic concerns to world leaders.

On this top-down front, Duchrow's primary concern is with global arrangements, and he strongly supports church-based activism to directly attack the existing multilateral institutions. Duchrow advocates debt relief for the Third World, and reviews a number of proposals to alter Bretton Woods Institutions, including exchange rate stabilization (see also Makhijani), stabilization of prices for basic commodities, a global income tax, tough national controls on capital flight, and mechanisms to enforce an international code of conduct for corporations. Duchrow as much as admits that the political plausibility of all these proposals is questionable in the coming period, but states that Christians and others have a moral obligation to push "political influence" on existing institutions as far as possible, while at the same time creating the "small-scaled" alternatives that can demonstrate the viability of an alternative to corporatist arrangements. Duchrow also provides four pages of exceptionally helpful charts reprinted from a now out-of-print book by American activist Bill Moyer describing the anatomy of successful social movements and four ways to be an effective activist—"citizen," "rebel," "change agent," or "reformer." These are contrasted to the multiple ways one can be politically ineffective—"naive citizen," "self-identity as a radical militant, a lonely voice on society's fringe," "cooptation," "tunnel vision," and a dozen other easily recognizable categories.

Duchrow thus meshes thorough analysis of "Biblical economics" with a critique of world economic arrangements and a working knowledge of alternative proposals. Duchrow does not, however, spell out a convincing strategy for how the experiments rooted in civil society and nongovernmental organizations might become the basis for a broader political strategy aimed at altering capitalism's basic institutions over time. Moreover, this book's focus on the Western European situation and Duchrow's rhetorical style (fraught with "should"s, "must"s and "it is imperative"s) place a limit on the book's appeal as an activist tool for Americans. It is to be hoped, however, that North Americans writing from a theological perspective can effectively blend the strengths of Duchrow's approach and his clear moral commitment in producing materials more suitable for American audiences, and at the same time re-engage some of the weak points of Duchrow's analysis.

Additional References

Charles Reich. *Opposing the System*. New York: Crown Publishers, 1995. Reich's book, aimed at a popular audience, urges Americans toward a "systemic" understanding of how corporations dominate American politics.

Charles Derber. *The Wilding of America*. New York: St. Martin's Press. 1996.

Charles Derber et al, *What's Left?* Amherst: University of Massachusetts Press, 1995. Derber is a respected left communitarian who has consistently related social breakdown and decay with economic inequality and corporate power. In *Wilding*, Derber develops a critique of current American culture's ratification of self-aggrandizement as a cultural norm; in *What's Left?*, Derber and his coauthors discuss historical and current precedents for building institutions and movements rooted in an ethos of solidarity, with special emphasis on the Mondragon cooperatives and the possibility of a "social market."

Boris Frankel. *The Post-Industrial Utopians*. Oxford: Polity Press, 1987. Hard-headed critique of the thought and proposals of Gorz, the Tofflers, Barry Jones, and Rudolf Bahro.

Jane Mansbridge. *Beyond Adversary Democracy*, New York: Basic Books, 1980. Usefully discusses how local-level "unitary democracy" —democracy rooted in discussion of the common good, not based on competing interests—could play a role in a reconstructed democratic system.

David Held. *Models of Democracy*, Stanford: Stanford University, 1987.. Title speaks for itself—useful academic exploration of different proposed forms of democracy.

Carol Gould. *Rethinking Democracy: Freedom and Social Cooperation in Politics, Economy and Society*. Cambridge: Cambridge University Press, 1988.

Stephen Elkin. *City and Regime in the American Republic*. Chicago: University of Chicago, 1987. Representative of a large literature in political science identifying how landholders and business interests dominate contemporary city politics.

Karol E. Soltan, and Stephen Elkin. *The Constitution of Good Societies*. University Park, PA: The Pennsylvania State University Press, 1996. Contributors include the editors, Elinor Ostrom, Viktor Vanberg and

James Buchanan, John Dryzek, Charles Anderson, Gar Alperovitz, and Philip Green. Publication of the Committee on the Political Economy of the Good Society, University of Maryland.

Francis Fukuyama. *The End of History and the Last Man.* New York: Free Press, 1991. Makes the claim that liberal democratic capitalism has proven its case as the ideal form for organizing the polity and the economy, given the collapse of socialist models.

Francis Moore Lappe and Paul DuBois. *The Quickening of America.* San Francisco: Jossey-Bass 1994. Study of various forms of community-building now evident at the grassroots in the United States.

Robert Schutz. *The $30,000 Solution.* Santa Barbara: Fithian Press, 1996. Falls into the category of utopian proposals from nonacademic writers; this book proposes distributing unearned income (including interest, rent, capital gains, dividends, inheritance, etc) to all Americans equally, plus adding a salary cap. The result, Schutz calculates, would be a guaranteed income of $30,000 a year for all Americans (before earned income).

Martin Tarcher. *Escape from Avarice.* Novato, CA: Chandler and Sharp Publishers, 1996. Tarcher provides a stringent critique, in essay form, of the present political-economic regime, and offers a series of proposed reforms in the direction of combining intelligent social planning with decentralization.

David Korten. *When Corporations Rule the World.* West Hartford, CT: Kumarian Press, 1995. Highly regarded study of the global ecological and economic crisis that squarely targets corporate power as the obstacle to people-centered development models, both in the developing world and the United States.

Leonardo Boff. *Ecology and Liberation: A New Paradigm.* Maryknoll, NY: Orbis Books, 1995. Boff, an important liberation theologian from Brazil, here connects his earlier Marx-informed analysis with ecological considerations.

Paul Hirst. *Associative Democracy: New Forms of Economic and Social Governance,* Amherst: University of Masachusetts, 1994. Like Cohen and Rogers, Hirst, who has been described as the "left wing" of the associative democracy shool, proposes citizen-based associations as the basis for certain forms of policy implementation as an alternative to the market and bureaucracy. This conception is envisioned as being strongly compatible with the development of cooperative grassroots economic institutions.

bell hooks. *Killing Rage: Ending Racism*. New York: H. Holt and Co., 1995. Essays on the intersection of feminist and anti-racist activism from a prominent theorist.

James Jennings, ed. *Race and Politics*. New York: Verso, 1997. Edited volume discussing the state of African-American activism and future strategies. Jennings endorse active Black participation in creating a new third party nationally.

Clarence J. Munford. *Race and Reparation: a Black Perspective for the 21st Century*. Trenton: Africa World Press, 1996. Spells out what a contemporary Black nationalist political program might look like.

Manning Marable. *Black Liberation in Conservative America*. Boston: South End Press, 1997. Collected essays from a prominent African-American socialist.

Kimberle Williams Crenshaw, ed. *Critical Race Theory*. New York: New Press, 1995. Edited volume of writings by leading African-American legal scholars illustrative of contemporary efforts to blend analysis of race and gender with critical legal studies. Little emphasis on constructive proposals.

Ellis Cose. *Color-Blind: Seeing Beyond Race in a Race-Obsessed World*. New York: HarperCollins, 1997. African-American journalist discusses the merits—and obstacles—to a strategy of integration.

Cornel West. *Race Matters*. Boston: Beacon Press, 1993. Collected essays on aspects of African-Americans' contemporary predicament; calls for a politics rooted in a "love ethic" as an antidote to "black nihilism."

Matthew Fox. *The Reinvention of Work: A New Vision of Livelihood for Our Time*. New York: Harper Collins, 1994. Useful discussion of how to bring new meaning and purpose into working life by a former Catholic priest.

Frithjoff Bergmann. *New Work*. Ann Arbor: Center for New Work, 1996. Bergmann, a philosopher at the University of Michigan, has been involved since the mid-1980s in projects in the Detroit area to create innovative working situations for laid-off auto workers whereby they work 6 months a year in the normal economy and can spend 6 months a year on personal skill development and other projects. This project and related concepts are covered in the book.

W.J. Conroy. *Challenging The Boundaries of Reform*. Philadelphia: Temple University Press, 1990. Study of municipal socialism under Bernie Sanders and others in Burlington, VT in the 1980s. Makes the novel proposal that American progressives should initiate a "state-by-state" long-term strategy by planned migration to Vermont, in order to turn it into a model state.

Jim Wallis. *The Soul of Politics*. New York: The New Press, 1994. Founder of the Sojourners Neighborhood Center in Washington, DC here fuses strongly progressive politics with evangelical Christianity to spell out a public ethic emphasizing both moral responsibility and social justice concerns; strongly oriented towards the build-up of local communities through economic alternatives.

Endnotes

1. Wolman and Colamosca, p. 216.

2. Greider, p. 325.

3. Faux, pp. 182-183.

4. Kuttner, p. 104.

5. Kuttner, p. 104.

6. Reich, *Locked in the Cabinet*, p. 184.

7. Reich, op. cit., p. 91.

8. Reich, op. cit., pp. 213-214.

9. Thurow, p. 42.

10. Thurow, p. 253.

11. Thurow, p. 270.

12. Galbraith, *The Culture of Contentment*, p. 182-183.

13. Galbraith, *The Good Society*, p. 139.

14. Bellah, *Habits of the Heart*, pp. 286-287.

15. Bellah, *Habits of the Heart*, p. 290.

16. Bellah, *The Good Society*, p. 108.

17. Sandel, pp. 215-216.

18. Sandel, p. 250.

19. Dionne, p. 304.

20. Wilson, p. 209.

21. Lind, *Up from Conservatism*, p. 244.

22. Lind, *The Next American Nation*, p. 144.

23. Blair, p. 86.

24. Blair, p. 90.

25. Shuman, from advance manuscript.

26. Meeker-Lowry, p. 213.

27. Brandt, p. 181.

28. Brandt, p. 199.

29. Stauber, *A New Program for Democratic Socialism*, p. 336, 351.

30. Stauber, *A New Program for Democratic Socialism*, p. 338.

31. Bardhan and Roemer, "Market Socialism: A Case for Rejuvenation." *Journal of Economic Perspectives*, Summer 1992. pp. 108-109.

32. Roemer, "John Roemer Replies." *Dissent*, Fall 1991. p. 573.

33. Bardhan and Roemer, op. cit. p. 112.

34. Roemer, "John Roemer Replies." *Dissent*, Fall 1991. p. 573.

35. Schweickart, p. 332.

36. Devine, "Market Socialism or Participatory Planning," p. 87.

37. McNally, p.181.

38. McNally, p. 187.

39. McNally, p. 184.

40. Brown, p. 397.

41. Bowles, Gordon, Weisskopf, *After the Wasteland*, pp. 207-208.

42. Brus and Laski, p. 147.

43. Arnold, p. 63.

44. Arnold, p. 62.

45. Pierson, p. 210.

46. Ophuls, *Ecology and the Politics of Scarcity,* p. 282.

47. Ophuls, p. 285.

48. Ophuls, pp. 286-87.

49. Ophuls, p. 287.

50. Ophuls, p. 287.

51. Ophuls, pp. 290-91.

52. Ophuls, p. 292.

53. Ophuls, p. 292.

54. Ophuls p. 315.

55. Bahro, p. 382.

56. Bahro, pp. 428-429.

57. Bahro, p. 430.

58. Frankel, Boris. *The Post-Industrial Utopians.* Madison: University of Wisconsin, 1987. p. 57.

59. Quoted in Frankel, op. cit., p. 30; see also Gorz, *Paths to Paradise*, p. 103.

60. Milbrath, p. 153.

61. Milbrath, p. 380.

62. Daly and Cobb, p. 235.

63. Daly and Cobb, p. 246.

64. Daly and Cobb, pp. 254-255.

65. Daly and Cobb, p. 258.

66. Daly and Cobb, p. 293.

67. Daly and Cobb, p. 331.

68. Trainer, *The Conserver Society*, p. 74.

69. Trainer, op. cit., p. 80.

70. Trainer, op.cit., p. 88.

71. Trainer, op.cit., p. 133.

72. Trainer, op.cit., p. 210.

73. Rasmussen, p. 351.

74. Bookchin, *From Urbanization to Cities*, p. 222.

75. Bookchin, *From Urbanization to Cities*, p. 235.

76. Bookchin, *From Urbanization to Cities*, p. 236.

77. Bookchin, *From Urbanization to Cities*, p. 266.

78. Callenbach, pp. 55-56.

79. Callenbach, p. 37.

80. LeGuin, p. 333.

81. Piercy, p. 105.

82. Moylan, p. 185.

83. Booker, pp. 142-146.

84. Atwood, p. 390.

85. Kennedy, p. 99.

86. Smith, p. 21.

87. Smith, p. 60, 85, 128.

88. Young, p. 253.

89. Cohen and Rogers, "Associations and Democracy," in Bardhan and Roemer, eds. *Market Socialism*. p. 238

90. Cohen and Rogers, "Associations and Democracy," in Bardhan and Roemer, eds. *Market Socialism*. p. 249.

91. Adams, from advance manuscript.

92. Adams, from advance manuscript.

93. Adams, from advance manuscript.

94. Dryzek, p. 147.

95. Dryzek, p. 150.

96. Dryzek, p. 148.

97. Dryzek, p. 154.

98. Naylor and Willimon, p. 284.

99. Fraser, p. 62.

100. Wells, p. 15, 49.

101. Barnet and Cavanagh, *Global Dreams*. New York: Simon and Schuster, 1994. p. 430.

102. Wells, p. 177.

103. Dorrien, p. 300.

104. Dorrien, p. 335.

105. Dorrien, p. 374.

106. Lerner, p. 285.

Thad Williamson has been a Research Associate at NCESA since 1992. He has written on disarmament, innovative economic strategies, and related issues for *Tikkun, The Nation, Monthly Review, Sojourners, Union Seminary Quarterly Review,* and other newspapers and periodicals. Williamson previously co-authored *The Index of Environmental Trends* (NCESA, 1995) and was a contributing researcher to Gar Alperovitz's *The Decision To Use the Atomic Bomb and the Architecture of an American Myth* (Knopf, 1995). He is currently enrolled as a graduate student at Union Theological Seminary in New York.

For more information contact:

The National Center for Economic and Security Alternatives
2000 P Street, NW, Suite 330
Washington, D.C. 20036, U.S.A.

tel: 202-835-1150   fax: 202-835-1152